simply
Salads

Editor: Jonathan Silverman
Layout and typesetting: Patty Holden
Cover: Patty Holden
Copy editing: Elizabeth Penn
Index preparation: Jonathan Silverman
Recipe consultation: Kelsey Lane

Printed in Hong Kong

ISBN 1-930603-66-5

Nutritional analysis computations
are approximate.

Table of Contents

Basics

Whether it's crisp greens, vegetables, sprouts, fruit, or cheese, there are few foods that can't be turned into a colorful, delicious salad. The only secret is the combination and quality of your ingredients. In the following pages, we'll teach you how to compose a wonderful salad and highlight a few of the key components that will come in handy when making any salad.

The first basic element of salad, one that all varieties have in common, is the dressing. It gives salads their character and unique flavor. A discussion of dressings should start with the key components of most dressing varieties—oil and vinegar.

Vinegar and Oil

There's an old saying: "It takes four people to dress a salad. A spendthrift for the oil, a miser for the vinegar, a sage for the salt and a madman to toss it."

But it's also possible to unite all these qualities in a single person if he or she takes the essence of this saying to heart. It isn't just a matter of quantities—the order of things is also important. You have to start by thoroughly mixing together salt, pepper, and vinegar and then whisk in the oil. The rest of what you need to know for making perfect dressings can be found on pages 12–16, but remember that vinegar isn't just vinegar and oil isn't just oil.

The varieties of vinegar available range greatly in both quality and cost. When composing salads with finer ingredients (e.g., meats, seafood, or fresh herbs), you should always reach for high-quality, aromatic vinegars. Today you can find these in any well-stocked supermarket and you can even make some special vinegars at home without too much trouble (see page 7).

The type of oil you use is a question of taste, health and, of course, your budget. Basically, extra virgin oils are recommended for salads. These varieties are rendered without heat and therefore yield a full-bodied taste. In the case of olive oil, extra virgin is sometimes referred to as cold-pressed. All extra virgin oils are especially rich in fat-soluble vitamin E as well as monounsaturated and polyunsaturated fatty acids. In contrast to the saturated fatty acids found in animal fat, these oils don't raise blood cholesterol and can even help to lower it.

Wine Vinegar

Read the label! If it says "distilled wine vinegar" it's just a blend of distilled vinegar and wine vinegar. If the label reads either "red," "white," or "champagne" wine vinegar, it's made from 100% pure grape wine. Bacteria have converted the alcohol in the wine to acetic acid. The acidity level must be at least 6%. Wine vinegar is aged in casks where it develops its typical aroma. Many salads acquire a refined flavor from good wine vinegar. The moderately tangy white wine vinegar is mainly suitable for vinaigrettes atop mild green salads, seafood, fish, and poultry. Slightly sweet, champagne vinegar marries well with salads containing fruit and or grilled or fried poultry. The strong, tart flavor of red wine vinegar goes well in salad dressings for hearty meats, lentils, and winter salad greens such as mâche.

Sherry Vinegar

In addition to its typical sherry flavor, this Spanish specialty often has a slightly nutty and woody aroma. Sherry vinegar that has been aged for an especially long time resembles balsamic vinegar (page 8) but is more subtle. Sherry vinegar is a fitting accompaniment to salads with hearty meats but also tastes great with celery, watercress, or oak leaf lettuce as well as fruit.

Apple Cider Vinegar

Almost all fruit vinegars are made from apples, from a base of hard apple cider or wine. The mild, fruity flavor goes very well with green salads and raw vegetables such as cabbage or carrots. The French cider vinegar is made from cider apples, has an especially intense flavor and goes very well with green beans or celery.

Herb Vinegar

A wide range of infused vinegars is available at many gourmet or natural foods markets. You can also make herb vinegar yourself without a lot of fuss. Suitable herbs include tarragon, thyme, dill, mint, and basil. Herb vinegar adds variety, especially in a vinaigrette for green salads.

SHORT RECIPE: Leave 2 herb sprigs, such as tarragon, in 2 cups good white wine vinegar stored at room temperature for 2–3 weeks. Then remove old sprigs and replace with fresh ones. It's best to put vinegar in a dark bottle. (Make sure the herbs are completely immersed in the vinegar. Toward the end of the 3 weeks or before use, remove the herbs so they don't mold.)

Raspberry and Strawberry Vinegars

These consist of a good wine vinegar infused with fruit or fruit essence. The combination of the sweetness of the fruit and acidity of the vinegar goes best with light summer salads (e.g., green salads or poultry).

SHORT RECIPE: For homemade raspberry vinegar, fill a bottle with 8 ounces fresh or frozen raspberries and 2 cups white wine vinegar and store at room temperature for about 3 weeks. Then pour vinegar through a sieve lined with cheesecloth or a coffee filter. Transfer to a bottle and seal.

Olive Oil

Olive oil contains a high percentage of monoun-saturated fatty acids and is the favorite of many a gourmet. There are fine distinctions in taste, depending on the origin, region, and type. Oil with an intense flavor goes well with salads containing tomatoes, bell peppers, zucchini, or eggplant and wherever garlic is involved. You can't always determine the intensity of flavor by looking at the color. Dark-green oil might well be mild whereas pale yellow oil can have a strong taste. There are three grades of olive oil that are precisely regulated by the International Olive Oil Council. The less free fatty acids (uniformly specified as oleic acidity), the better—and the more expensive—the oil. The highest quality, extra virgin, is produced from the first pressing and tends to be light-green with a fine flavor. Virgin oil comes from the second pressing. If the label says only "olive oil," it is a blend of virgin oil and refined (chemically purified) or unrefined oil, which involves heating the olives to extract the oil.

SHORT RECIPE: For garlic oil, place 3 peeled garlic cloves and 1 cup olive oil in a bottle and store for 2 weeks at room temperature. Ideal for vinaigrettes, mayonnaise, and browning croutons.

Lemon Vinegar

This fine blend of acetic and citric acids goes especially well with crudités. You can buy ready-made lemon vinegar but it's also easy to make it yourself.

SHORT RECIPE: Thoroughly rinse 1 lemon. Then combine grated zest and 1 cup white wine vinegar in a bottle and refrigerate for three weeks.

Balsamic Vinegar

Genuine "Aceto Balsamico Traditionale" is produced only in extremely small quantities in Italy's Modena region and costs a fortune. It is aged at least 12 years before arriving in specialty stores. It starts out with the reduced "must" of trebianno grapes that is aged through a very complicated procedure in special wooden casks, resulting in a sweet and sour, intensely flavored elixir. The balsamic vinegar in large bottles that you find in supermarkets at a somewhat lower price is aged for a much shorter period of time. This vinegar, also sold as "Aceto Balsamico di Modena," can still be a great enhancement to your salads. Balsamic vinegar is suitable for hearty vinaigrettes: tomatoes, arugula, poultry, or lentils, but can also lend a special accent to fruit salads.

The number of special vinegars is immense: Some worth mentioning are rice wine vinegar for Asian salads, honey vinegar for green salads and crudités, malt vinegar for cabbage and radish salads, and cane vinegar for Caribbean dishes.

Sunflower Oil

This light-yellow to dark-yellow oil derived from sunflower seeds is rich in polyunsaturated fatty acids and vitamin E. It's flavor varies from mild to neutral. Sunflower oil is ideal for crudités and goes with any green salad.

Corn Oil

This oil has no distinct aroma. It is derived from ripe, chopped corn and has a neutral flavor. With regard to fatty acids, it's a good choice for making healthy salads and is suitable for all salads that have their own distinctive flavor (e.g., celery root).

Safflower Oil

This oil is derived from safflower seeds. The proportion of polyunsaturated fatty acids and vitamin E is especially high, which yields a nutritious oil with a mildly bitter flavor that goes with all green salads.

Pumpkin Seed Oil

This specialty from the Austrian province of Styria is rich in polyunsaturated fatty acids and has a powerful flavor. The oil varies from dark-green to black. It is derived from the seeds of special oil pumpkins and goes particularly well with crudités, potato, or beef salads and those with white beans.

Grape Seed Oil

This light-colored, slightly greenish oil is pressed from the seeds of grapes and is rich in polyunsaturated fatty acids and vitamin E. Its mild, slightly nutty flavor is excellent in dressings for crudités and salads with roasted meat.

Walnut and Hazelnut Oils

Both of these nut oils have an intense flavor and are full of nutritious unsaturated fatty acids. They go well with hearty greens such as frisée and oak leaf lettuce as well as salads containing nuts. If you want a less intense flavor, you can also dilute walnut or hazelnut oil with a neutral oil.

Wheat Germ Oil

This oil has the highest vitamin E content and a high percentage of polyunsaturated fatty acids. It has a flavor reminiscent of grain. Wheat germ oil is best with crudités and green salads.

Sesame Oil

This oil, most commonly golden-yellow but also available in a darker, toasted variety, is rich in mono- and polyunsaturated fatty acids and has the nutty flavor of roasted sesame seeds. It should be used sparingly or mixed with other oils and goes especially well in Asian salads.

Canola Oil

This oil is rich in mono- and polyunsaturated fatty acids as well as vitamin E. Due to its rough flavor, it was once less popular but new types of rape plant now provide a pleasant, neutral-tasting varietal.

How can you clean and cut up tender salad greens without losing a lot of the vitamins? A perfect salad requires suitable tools, the expertise to handle the raw ingredients correctly, and the composition of a dressing to bring them all together. Below, you will find steps for bringing greens from the farm to your salad bowl, while maintaining their color, flavor, and nutritional value.

Preparing Salad Greens and Herbs

Salad greens must be handled with care if they're to stay crisp and retain essential vitamins. The basic rule is: first rinse, then cut. Never leave the greens in water for too long and never in warm water, otherwise their water-soluble vitamins and minerals end up going down the drain. Always cut herbs at the last minute so they won't lose their body and flavor.

Cleaning and Rinsing Greens

In the case of butterhead lettuce, first remove the outer wilted or damaged leaves and then cut out the core with a small knife.

Next remove the individual leaves and move them around briefly in a bowl of cold water. Follow the same procedure for escarole, frisée, oak leaf, romaine, etc. Make sure that the bowl is deep enough so that the dirt that settles at the bottom is not constantly stirred up by the lettuce leaves. In the case of greens that will subsequently be cut up into eighths or strips such as iceberg lettuce or radicchio, remove a generous portion of outer leaves and then rinse both the leaves and the part of the head still intact under running water.

Mâche must be cleaned especially well. Cut the small roots from the rosettes in such a way that the leaves stay together. Remove wilted leaves. Then rinse several times in cold water until no more sand washes out. For mâche with especially large leaves, divide into individual leaves.

Spinning Greens Dry

A perfect green salad requires that the leaves be carefully dried. Wet leaves water down the dressing, and the dressing doesn't adhere to them as well. The fastest and simplest method is to use a wire basket that you take by the handle and spin it back and forth at a high speed over the sink, thereby removing most of the water.

You can use a closed salad spinner, available in plastic or stainless steel from any kitchen or department store.

If you don't have a special device, place the leaves in a clean dishtowel and spin them dry in the cloth. In a pinch you can also shake them dry in a standard colander but it's a relatively long process.

Cutting Up Greens

Whole lettuce leaves (e.g., butterhead or escarole): Cut off thick ends of ribs. Coarsely tear up large leaves.

Strips such as iceberg, endive, or radicchio: Cut head in half, cut out wedge-shaped core, and cut greens into strips.

TIP: Many specialty kitchen stores carry plastic lettuce knives. Using these as opposed to steel knives can prevent browning of lettuce leaves.

Divide romaine lettuce into leaves, rinse, and spin dry, then stack about 6–7 leaves on top of one another and cut into strips.

Lettuce leaves used to decoratively line salad plates, such as endive or radicchio: Cut head in half and quarters if desired and cut out hard core with a paring knife.

Rinsing and Cutting Up Herbs

Rinse herbs under cold running water, then dry well, either by patting them with paper towels or by shaking them with your hands and then letting them dry on paper towels.

It's best to cut up large-leaved herbs (e.g., basil or mint) on a cutting board using a knife. Remove leaves from stems, stack them on top of one another, and cut them into strips, also called chiffonade.

For small and very feathery leaves (e.g., parsley, dill, or chervil) a mezzaluna or crescent knife is ideal. Remove leaves from stems and chop, preferably on a special board with a well.

For small amounts of herbs, scissors can also be very practical. They allow you to cut the herbs directly over the salad bowl (e.g., chives). Special scissors are available for herbs but you can also use conventional kitchen scissors.

The dressing is the soul of any salad. Here you will find basic recipes for the classics—from vinaigrette and mayonnaise to yogurt dressing. Each type of dressing is subject to many variations so let your imagination run wild!

All dressings need to be mixed well. Immediately prior to serving, any dressing you prepare must either be whisked thoroughly in a bowl or shaken up in its sealed storage container.

Depending on the type of salad (e.g., green or pasta salad), toss the ingredients with the dressing in a large bowl using a salad fork and spoon set. In the case of appetizer salads, the ingredients are often arranged on plates, then drizzled with dressing and served. Another option for salads that wilt quickly is to serve the undressed salad with the dressing on the side so that each person can dress their own. In this case, be sure to provide a lot of dressing because people generally tend to serve themselves liberally.

Vinaigrette

The main ingredients in vinaigrette are oil and vinegar. The vinaigrette originated in France and its character is determined by the type of oil and vinegar used. Traditionally, it's made with wine vinegar and olive oil. The usual ratio is 1 part vinegar to 4 parts oil but this can, of course, be varied according to individual taste. If you want, rub the inside of the salad bowl with a half clove of garlic beforehand and mix in 1 finely diced shallot. A finely chopped hard-boiled egg also goes well with many basic vinaigrettes.

Vinaigrette is extremely versatile. It goes with all salad greens, tomato and cucumber salads, bean and potato salads, artichokes, and asparagus. It also makes a superior marinade for meat or fish as long as the protein does not spend too much time in the acetic acid of the vinegar.

Basic Vinaigrette

Serves 4:
½ teaspoon Dijon mustard
2 tablespoons white wine vinegar
Salt (preferably kosher or sea)
White pepper
6 tablespoons oil (e.g., sunflower oil)
1 tablespoon chopped herbs
(e.g., chives, parsley, chervil, dill, tarragon)

Using a wire whisk, beat mustard, vinegar, salt, and pepper in a bowl until the salt is completely dissolved.

Whisk in the oil and continue mixing until all the ingredients have merged and the dressing is smooth. Then stir in herbs.

TIP: Vinaigrette is great for making in larger quantities and keeps for weeks. Combine ½ cup vinegar, 2 cups oil, salt, and pepper and store in a tightly sealed bottle. Before adding to a salad, shake the dressing well in the bottle because the oil settles to the bottom. Then pour the desired amount over your salad and mix in fresh, chopped herbs.

French Vinaigrette

Serves 4:
½ teaspoon Dijon mustard
2 tablespoons white wine vinegar
1–2 tablespoons white wine or 2 tablespoons lemon juice
Salt (preferably kosher or sea)
White pepper
4 tablespoons oil (e.g., sunflower)
2 tablespoons walnut oil
1 tablespoon chopped herbs (e.g., parsley, chervil)

Preparation is the same as for vinaigrette except that white wine or lemon juice is added with the other ingredients.

Goes especially well with green salads.

Italian Dressing

Serves 4:
½ teaspoon Dijon mustard
1 tablespoon white wine vinegar
1 tablespoon balsamic vinegar
Salt (preferably kosher or sea)
White pepper
6 tablespoons extra virgin olive oil
2 sprigs basil

Whisk together ingredients as described for the vinaigrette. Then rinse basil, cut leaves into strips, and stir into vinaigrette.

Goes especially well with a tomato salad.

Spanish Dressing

Serves 4:
½ teaspoon Dijon mustard
2 tablespoons sherry vinegar
2 tablespoons freshly squeezed orange juice
Salt (preferably kosher or sea)
White pepper
6 tablespoons extra virgin olive oil

Stir together mustard, sherry vinegar, orange juice, salt, and pepper and then whisk in oil.

Goes especially well with avocados or celery root.

Mayonnaise

Homemade mayonnaise can make a salad decadent and is quite different from the bottled varieties you'll find in the store. The important thing is that the eggs are very fresh. All the ingredients should be at room temperature before you begin.

Mayonnaise goes with heartier salads made with pasta, fish, seafood, potatoes, poultry, artichokes, endive, celeriac, and cauliflower.

Serves 4–6:
½ teaspoon Dijon mustard
1 fresh egg yolk
Salt (preferably kosher or sea)
White pepper
1 tablespoon lemon juice
½ cup olive or sunflower oil

Whisk mustard, egg yolk, salt, pepper, and lemon juice with a whisk attachment on an electric hand mixer or a wire whisk.

Stir in about 2 tablespoons oil drop by drop while continuing to beat vigorously.

Add remaining oil in a thin stream and continue beating until the dressing has a smooth, consistent texture.

TIPS: In a tightly sealed container, mayonnaise keeps in the refrigerator for about 1 week.

If you're in a hurry, you can also use mayonnaise from a jar. Salad mayonnaise contains 50% fat so use it sparingly. These days, however, you can also buy many types of reduced-fat mayonnaise and mayonnaise-like dressings that contain less fat because they are made with fat substitutes like yogurt.

VARIATIONS:

Herb mayonnaise: Stir 3 tablespoons finely chopped herbs into the mayonnaise.

Garlic mayonnaise: Squeeze 2 peeled garlic cloves through a press and add.

Thousand Island Dressing

Serves 4–6:
½ teaspoon Dijon mustard
1 fresh egg yolk
Salt (preferably kosher or sea)
White pepper
1 tablespoon white wine vinegar
½ cup olive or sunflower oil
½ red bell pepper, finely diced
1 small pickle, finely chopped
3 tablespoons tomato ketchup
½ teaspoon Hungarian sweet paprika
1 pinch cayenne pepper

Prepare mayonnaise as described above. Then stir in bell pepper, pickle, and ketchup. Season to taste with paprika and cayenne.

Remoulade

Serves 4:
1½ teaspoons Dijon mustard
1 fresh egg yolk
Salt (preferably kosher or sea)
White pepper
1 tablespoon white wine vinegar
½ cup olive or sunflower oil
1 hard-boiled egg, finely chopped
1 ounce chopped pickles
1 tablespoon finely chopped parsley
2 ounces capers (optional)

Prepare mayonnaise as described above, then stir in egg, pickles, parsley, and capers.

Yogurt Dressing

Dressings with yogurt and lemon juice are especially light and refreshing. If you want, you can add garlic squeezed through a press.

Yogurt dressing is as well suited to green salads as to crudités and pasta salads. It also goes very well with salads containing fruit.

Serves 4:
6 ounces plain yogurt
2 tablespoons lemon juice
1 tablespoon sunflower or corn oil
Salt (preferably kosher or sea)
White pepper
2 tablespoons chopped herbs
(e.g., chives, parsley, dill, lemon balm)

Beat yogurt, lemon juice, and oil with a wire whisk until creamy. Season to taste with salt, pepper, and herbs.

VARIATION:
Sour cream dressing: Instead of yogurt, use 6 ounces sour cream (10% fat)

Cheese Dressing

Cheese gives your dressing a dominant flavor. Creamy cheese dressings are usually served on the side and not tossed with the salad. If you want you can mix in chopped herbs such as parsley, dill, or chervil. Cheese dressings are excellent with celery, endive, or iceberg lettuce.

Serves 4:
2 ounces Roquefort or Gorgonzola
5 tablespoons heavy cream
3 tablespoons sunflower or corn oil
2 tablespoons white wine vinegar
Salt (preferably kosher or sea)
White pepper

Mash cheese with a fork and mix with cream, oil, and vinegar until the dressing has a smooth, creamy texture. Season dressing to taste with salt and pepper.

VARIATION:
Goat Cheese (Chévre) Dressing: Instead of Roquefort, use 2 ounces goat cheese and replace the vinegar with lemon juice. The resulting dressing tastes much milder so you can flavor it with chopped herbs.

Leafy Salads

Iceberg Lettuce

with Lemon Cream or Olive Dressing

with Lemon Cream

Serves 4:
For the lemon cream:
1 lemon
1 clove garlic
1 shallot
2 tablespoons sunflower or corn oil
2 ounces Alouette (or any soft, spreadable cheese)
6 ounces crème fraîche
1 pinch powdered sugar
Salt (preferably kosher or sea)
White pepper
For the salad:
1 bunch dill
2 small, firm heads of iceberg lettuce
Dill flowers (optional)

Prep time: 25 minutes
Per serving approx: 239 calories
5 g protein/21 g fat/13 g carbohydrates

For the lemon cream, wash lemon thoroughly and remove zest with a zester. Cut lemon in half and squeeze juice into a bowl. Peel garlic and squeeze through a press. Peel shallot and dice very finely.

Combine lemon juice, oil, garlic, and shallot. Beat together Alouette and crème fraîche, then stir into the lemon dressing. Add lemon zest and season to taste with powdered sugar, salt, and pepper.

Rinse dill and separate into sprigs. Clean lettuce, rinse thoroughly, spin dry, and tear leaves into bite-sized pieces. Distribute lettuce on four plates and pour lemon cream over the top. Sprinkle with dill sprigs. Garnish with dill flowers if desired.

Serve as a side dish with fish entrées.

with Olive Dressing

Serves 4:
1 small onion
2 cloves garlic
3 ounces black olives
1 tablespoon fresh thyme leaves
Salt (preferably kosher or sea)
Freshly ground black pepper
2 tablespoons red wine vinegar
6 tablespoons extra virgin olive oil
1 red bell pepper
1 yellow bell pepper
½ head iceberg lettuce

Prep time: 30 minutes
Per serving approx: 244 calories
2 g protein/23 g fat/10 g carbohydrates

For the dressing, peel and chop onion and garlic. Remove pits from 1 ounce olives (preferably with a cherry pitter) and chop olives. Mix these ingredients together with thyme, salt, pepper, and vinegar, then whisk in olive oil. Season dressing to taste.

Cut bell peppers in half, rinse, clean, and cut into narrow strips.

Clean iceberg lettuce, rinse leaves, spin dry, and cut into 1½-inch strips.

Arrange lettuce and pepper strips on plates, drizzle with olive dressing, and sprinkle with remaining olives.

Serve as a side with grilled fish.

Escarole with Creamy Dressing

Serves 4:
2 pink grapefruit
1 head escarole
5 tablespoons pecans
For the dressing:
3 ounces heavy cream
4 ounces crème fraîche
Salt (preferably kosher or sea)
White pepper
¼ teaspoon sugar

Prep time: 30 minutes
Per serving approx: 203 calories
3 g protein/19 g fat/6 g carbohydrates

Rinse grapefruit. Carefully peel over a bowl, also removing the white, outer membrane. Peel each section so you have just the flesh, but make sure to catch the dripping juice in the bowl.

Clean escarole, rinse, spin dry, and tear into smaller pieces. Coarsely chop 3 tablespoons pecans.

For the dressing, whisk 3 tablespoons of the grapefruit juice you saved, heavy cream and crème fraîche with a wire whisk until slightly foamy. Season to taste with salt, pepper, and sugar.

Toss escarole with dressing or drizzle dressing over the top and arrange with grapefruit sections. Sprinkle with chopped pecans and garnish with remaining whole pecans.

Serve as a side dish with grilled foods.

Oak Leaf Lettuce with Walnut Cheese Rounds

Serves 4:

For the cheese rounds:
4 ounces goat cheese
3 ounces Camembert (55% fat)
Salt (preferably kosher or sea)
Freshly ground black pepper
1 teaspoon lemon juice
2–3 tablespoons walnuts

For the dressing:
2 tablespoons white
wine vinegar
1 heaping teaspoon
Dijon mustard
Salt (preferably kosher or sea)
Freshly ground black pepper

5 tablespoons sunflower
or corn oil
2 tablespoons walnut oil

For the salad:
1 head oak leaf lettuce
(about 7 ounces)
Several sprigs watercress
1 tablespoon chopped walnuts

Prep time: 30 minutes
(+ 1–2 hours refrigeration time)
Per serving approx: 341 calories
9 g protein/31 g fat/6 g carbohydrates

Fold aluminum foil over the plastic wrap and cheese mixture.

Roll cheese mixture back and forth in the foil to shape it into a cylinder.

Put goat cheese in a large soup bowl. Using a sharp knife, shave rind from Camembert if desired and add Camembert to goat cheese. Mash together two cheeses thoroughly with a fork. Season to taste with salt, pepper, and lemon juice.

Heap the cheese mixture on a sheet of plastic wrap. Fold plastic over the top and roll cheese mixture on the work surface until you have a roll with a diameter of 1 inch. Tightly wrap the plastic in aluminum foil and refrigerate 1–2 hours.

For the vinaigrette, whisk vinegar, mustard, salt, and pepper. Then gradually whisk in both types of oil.

Clean lettuce, rinse, spin dry, and tear into bite-sized pieces. For the cheese rounds, coarsely grind all the walnuts in a blender or food processor.

Carefully roll the refrigerated cheese in the walnuts.

Spread out the walnuts on the work surface. Unwrap the cheese roll and carefully roll it over the nuts, allowing the walnuts to evenly coat the outside of the cheese.

Immediately cut the roll into slices no more than ½-inch thick. Toss oak leaf with vinaigrette and arrange on four plates along with cheese rounds. Rinse and cut watercress from stems. Garnish salad with watercress and chopped walnuts left over from cheese.

TIPS: Instead of the refrigerator, you can place the cheese roll in the freezer for 30 minutes.

If you don't have any walnuts, this salad is also excellent with sesame seeds: Roast 3–4 tablespoons sesame seeds in a nonstick pan until golden brown and let cool. Spread out 2–3 tablespoons of these on a work surface and roll the cheese roll in them. Set aside the rest for garnish. For the vinaigrette, substitute 1 tablespoon sesame oil (its flavor is very intense) for the 2 tablespoons walnut oil.

Serves 4:
1 sprig rosemary
4 ounces mild feta
1 pickled chile pepper
2 tablespoons apple cider vinegar
Sea salt
Freshly ground black pepper
1 pinch mustard powder
5 tablespoons extra virgin olive oil
½ head escarole
½ head oak leaf lettuce
¼ head romaine lettuce
4 ripe yellow star fruit (14 ounces)
1 nectarine
8 walnut halves

Prep time: 40 minutes
Per serving approx: 321 calories
6 g protein/26 g fat/19 g carbohydrates

Rinse rosemary, strip needles from stem, and chop finely. Cut feta into small cubes and sprinkle with rosemary. Slit open chile pepper, scrape out seeds, cut into thin strips, and sprinkle on feta.

For the dressing, mix vinegar, salt, pepper, and mustard, then whisk in oil.

Clean lettuce, separate into leaves, rinse, and spin dry. Rinse star fruit and nectarine and dry. Slice star fruit. Cut nectarine in half, remove pit, and cut into thin wedges.

Heat a nonstick pan over medium heat without oil. In the meantime, tear lettuce leaves into smaller pieces and toss with the prepared dressing in a bowl, then add fruit to the bowl. Roast walnuts in the pan and sprinkle over salad. Then transfer cheese to the pan, heat without letting it melt and distribute it over the salad.

TIP: Depending on your taste for spice, you can use a milder or hotter chile pepper. You can also use a milder or hotter mustard powder.

Serves 4:
2 stalks celery
1 small fennel bulb with greens
1 ounce pine nuts
1 head romaine lettuce
2 ounces freshly shaved Parmesan
For the dressing:
2 scallions
2 tablespoons balsamic vinegar
2 tablespoons extra virgin olive oil
1 tablespoon pine nut oil or another nut oil
Salt (preferably kosher or sea)
White pepper

Prep time: 30 minutes
Per serving approx: 179 calories
10 g protein/13 g fat/10 g carbohydrates

Rinse celery, cut off leaves, and remove tough fibers from the stalks. Cut stalks into small cubes. Rinse fennel bulb, clean, and cut in half lengthwise. Remove fennel greens and set aside. Remove core from fennel halves and cut fennel crosswise against the grain into fine strips. Roast pine nuts in a nonstick pan without oil and set aside.

For the dressing, clean scallions, cut in half lengthwise, rinse, and dice finely. In a bowl, whisk together scallions and vinegar. Add two types of oil, salt and pepper, and stir vigorously. Add additional salt and pepper to taste.

Clean romaine and separate into leaves. Rinse leaves thoroughly, spin dry, and tear into smaller pieces. Combine romaine, fennel, and celery in a large salad bowl and toss with dressing. Sprinkle with shaved Parmesan and pine nuts. Garnish with fennel greens.

Serve as an appetizer or as a small snack with a baguette and prosciutto.

Cheese & Fried Potato Salad

Serves 4:
1 bunch mixed herbs (e.g., parsley, dill, tarragon, chervil)
1 ounce unsalted cashews
4 ounces goat cheese
3 ounces sour cream
1 clove garlic
Sea salt
Freshly ground black pepper
2 ounces heavy cream
2 fresh egg whites
4 teaspoons balsamic vinegar
4 tablespoons extra virgin olive oil
½ teaspoon thyme leaves
1 pound russet potatoes
1 tablespoon chopped rosemary
4 ounces arugula
½ head frisée lettuce
2 ounces radicchio
¼ each of a red, green, and yellow bell pepper
Several thyme flowers (optional)

Prep time: 45 minutes
(+ 2 hours refrigeration time)
Per serving approx: 432 calories
17 g protein/31 g fat/24 g carbohydrates

Rinse and chop herbs. Along with cashews, process herbs into a paste using a blender or food processor, and transfer to a bowl. Add cheese and sour cream and mix well. Peel garlic, squeeze through a press, add, and stir. Season cheese mixture generously to taste with salt and pepper.

Add 1 pinch salt to cream and 1 pinch salt to egg whites and beat each separately until stiff. Then fold both into cheese mixture. Cover and refrigerate for 2 hours.

After 1½ hours, start the dressing. Mix vinegar, salt, and pepper and then stir in 2 tablespoons oil. Stir in thyme. For the fried potatoes, rinse potatoes, peel, and grate coarsely. Combine with rosemary, salt, and pepper. For the salad, clean arugula, frisée, and radicchio, rinse and spin dry. Clean bell peppers, rinse, and cut into small cubes.

In a wide pan, heat remaining oil over medium heat. With a spoon, set four piles of grated potatoes in the pan and press down slightly on each (they shouldn't touch one another). Fry potatoes for 5 minutes on each side until golden brown.

Tear lettuce leaves into bite-size pieces, toss with dressing, and distribute on four plates. Cut potato pancakes into quarters, distribute on plates, and top each one with 2 heaping tablespoons goat cheese cream. Sprinkle with bell pepper confetti. Garnish with thyme flowers if desired.

Endive & Escarole with Cheese Dressing

Serves 4:
2 heads white endive (about 10 ounces)
4 ounces escarole
4 ounces cherry tomatoes
1 shallot
3 ounces Roquefort
5 ounces crème fraîche
3 tablespoons lemon juice
1 teaspoon Cognac (optional)
2 tablespoons chopped chives
Salt (preferably kosher or sea)
Freshly ground black pepper
10 whole chives

Prep time: 30 minutes
Per serving approx: 243 calories
6 g protein/18 g fat/14 g carbohydrates

Clean endive and escarole, rinse, spin dry, and cut or tear leaves into smaller pieces. Rinse tomatoes and slice or cut in half. Combine with lettuce in a bowl or arrange decoratively on plates. Peel shallot, dice finely, and sprinkle over the top.

Mash cheese thoroughly with a fork. Combine with crème fraîche, lemon juice, Cognac (if desired), and chopped chives. Season dressing with salt and pepper and pour over the lettuce, but don't toss. Garnish with whole chives.

TIP: If desired, garnish with a few slices of Roquefort.

Herb Salad with Sautéed Mushrooms

Serves 4:
6 ounces fresh mushrooms (e.g., chanterolle, white button, shiitake)
1 onion
4 tablespoons sunflower or corn oil
1 teaspoon soy sauce
1 teaspoon medium-hot mustard
2 tablespoons sherry vinegar
1 tablespoon walnut or hazelnut oil
Salt (preferably kosher or sea)
Freshly ground black pepper
2 sprigs fresh oregano (with flowers if desired)
12 ounces mixed leaf lettuce (e.g., red leaf, oak leaf, escarole, mâche)

Prep time: 35 minutes
Per serving approx: 219 calories
5 g protein/10 g fat/34 g carbohydrates

Wipe off mushrooms with a paper towel. Clean chanterelles and shiitake thoroughly and remove shiitake stems. Slice white mushrooms. Peel onion and chop finely.

In a pan, heat 2 tablespoons sunflower or corn oil. Sauté onion briefly over medium heat. Add mushrooms and brown for 2–3 minutes. Season with soy sauce and set aside.

For the salad dressing, thoroughly mix together mustard, sherry vinegar, remaining oil, and nut oil. Season with salt and pepper. Briefly rinse oregano and remove leaves from stems.

Clean lettuce, rinse thoroughly, and spin dry. Place in a bowl and toss with dressing.

Distribute mushrooms on salad and sprinkle with oregano leaves. If desired, garnish with oregano flowers.

Arugula Frisée Salad

Serves 4:
1 bunch frisée
2 ounces arugula
1 carrot (about 4 ounces)
1 whole grain roll
2 ounces butter, unsalted
1 clove garlic
Sea salt
3 tablespoons herb vinegar
½ teaspoon honey
Freshly ground black pepper
6 tablespoons safflower oil
1 handful alfalfa sprouts

Prep time: 30 minutes
Per serving approx: 254 calories
3 g protein/22 g fat/14 g carbohydrates

Clean frisée, rinse, spin dry, and tear up tender tips of leaves. Slice stems finely and on an angle. Sort arugula, clean, rinse, and spin dry. Clean carrot, peel, and grate coarsely.

Cut roll in half and slice thinly. In a pan, heat butter. Peel garlic, squeeze through a press, and add to pan. Toast bread and garlic until golden brown. Season with salt and let cool.

For the dressing, place vinegar, honey, salt, and pepper in a bowl and whisk together with oil. Add frisée, arugula, and grated carrot, toss, and arrange on plates. Rinse sprouts briefly and shake dry. Sprinkle salad with bread and sprouts.

TIP: Instead of grating the carrot, you can also slice it thinly and then punch out shapes with a cookie or other kitchen cutter to give them added visual appeal.

Serves 4:
2 tablespoons balsamic vinegar
1 teaspoon medium-hot mustard
¼ teaspoon coarsely crushed black pepper
4 tablespoons extra virgin olive oil
6 ounces arugula
3 ounces sorrel
1 bunch mixed herbs (e.g., tarragon, chervil, parsley)
½ bunch basil
1 ounce watercress
1 head green leaf lettuce
1 ounce pine nuts
7 ounces cherry tomatoes
1 beet
⅓ cucumber

Prep time: 30 minutes
Per serving approx: 318 calories
4 g protein/31 g fat/10 g carbohydrates

In a bowl, mix together vinegar, mustard, and pepper, then whisk in oil. Clean arugula, sorrel, mixed herbs, basil, watercress, and green leaf lettuce. Separate lettuce into leaves. Rinse all greens and spin dry. Then remove herb leaves from stems.

Heat a pan and roast pine nuts without oil until golden brown. Set aside.

Rinse tomatoes, beet, and cucumber. Cut tomatoes in half. Peel raw beet, clean, and cut into thin (julienne) strips. Peel cucumber and dice.

Toss lettuce and herbs with vinaigrette. Loosely fold in tomatoes, beet, and cucumber. Sprinkle with pine nuts.

Sorrel Salad with Almonds

Serves 4:
1 sprig Itallan parsley
2 tablespoons balsamic vinegar
1 teaspoon medium-hot mustard
Sea salt
Freshly ground black pepper
4 tablespoons extra virgin olive oil
1 small zucchini
1 small carrot
10 ounces sorrel
¼ head red leaf lettuce
¼ head escarole
12 almonds
4 mushrooms
Several whole chives

Prep time: 30 minutes
Per serving approx: 134 calories
4 g protein/10 g fat/9 g carbohydrates

For the dressing, rinse parsley and chop leaves finely. Thoroughly mix vinegar, mustard, salt, pepper, and parsley and then whisk in oil.

Rinse zucchini and carrot, clean, and cut into matchsticks with a vegetable slicer or julienne by hand. Add to dressing.

Sort sorrel, cut off stems, rinse, spin dry, and tear larger leaves into smaller pieces. Clean red leaf lettuce and escarole, separate into leaves, rinse, spin dry, and tear into smaller pieces.

In a small pot, bring water to a boil and boil almonds for 1–2 minutes. Drain and remove skins. Wipe mushrooms with a dry cloth and slice thinly.

Toss sorrel and leaf lettuce with dressing and distribute on plates. Top decoratively with mushrooms, almonds, and whole chives.

Vegetable Salads

Cucumber Mushroom Salad

Serves 4:
2 shallots
1 clove garlic
8 ounces spinach
1 tablespoon olive oil
Salt (preferably kosher or sea)
Freshly ground black pepper
12 ounces cucumber
8 ounces large white mushrooms
4 ounces feta
For the dressing:
1 small bunch dill
2 tablespoons white wine vinegar
Salt (preferably kosher or sea)
Freshly ground black pepper
6 tablespoons extra virgin olive oil

Prep time: 40 minutes
Per serving approx: 220 calories
7 g protein/19 g fat/10 g carbohydrates

Peel shallots and garlic and dice finely. Sort spinach, clean, rinse, and chop coarsely. In a pot, heat olive oil and sauté shallots and garlic until translucent. Add spinach while still wet, season with salt and pepper, and cook for 1 minute while stirring. Cover pot and set aside.

Rinse cucumber thoroughly and peel if desired. Slice thinly. Wipe mushrooms with a dry cloth, clean, and slice. Distribute mushrooms and cucumber on one large platter or on plates.

For the dressing, rinse dill and chop leaves. Mix together with vinegar, salt, and pepper, then thoroughly whisk in oil. Season dressing to taste and drizzle over cucumber and mushroom slices.

Season lukewarm spinach to taste and transfer to center of platter or plates. Dice feta and sprinkle over salad. Grind pepper over the top.

TIP: For a special occasion, you can also add a few marinated squid to the salad.

#
Asparagus & Herb Salad

Serves 4:
2¼ pounds green asparagus
8 ounces sugar snap peas
Salt (preferably kosher or sea)
Sugar
For the herb vinaigrette:
1 shallot
½ teaspoon medium-hot mustard
Salt (preferably kosher or sea)
2 tablespoons white wine vinegar
1 tablespoon sherry vinegar
2 tablespoons chopped, mixed herbs
(e.g., tarragon, chervil, chives)
3 tablespoons sunflower oil
2 tablespoons walnut oil
1 hard-boiled egg (optional)
White pepper

Prep time: 40 minutes
(+1 hour marinating time)
Per serving approx: 152 calories
6 g protein/11 g fat/10 g carbohydrates

Peel bottom of asparagus spears and cut off woody ends. Clean sugar snap peas, rinse, and cut in half if desired. In a wide pot, bring 1 gallon water to a boil with a little salt and sugar. Blanch peas 2½–5 minutes. Remove, rinse under cold water, and drain. Then add asparagus to pot, cover, and simmer over low heat for 10 minutes. Remove asparagus from water, drain, cover, and let cool.

For the herb vinaigrette, peel shallot and mince. Combine 2 tablespoons asparagus water, mustard, and salt. Add the two types of vinegar and herbs and mix thoroughly. Whisk in two types of oil. If desired, peel egg, chop finely, and stir into vinaigrette. Season to taste with salt and pepper.

Transfer asparagus and peas to a platter or bowl. Pour herb vinaigrette over the top. Cover, marinate for 1 hour, and serve.

Serves 4–6:
For the herb dip:
1 bunch Italian parsley
2 sprigs basil
1 clove garlic
2 anchovy fillets
2 tablespoons capers
2 tablespoons lemon juice
$\frac{1}{2}$ cup extra virgin olive oil
3 tablespoons fresh breadcrumbs
Salt (preferably kosher or sea)
Freshly ground black pepper
For the lemon aioli:
1 lemon
1 egg yolk
Salt (preferably kosher or sea)
1 teaspoon medium-hot mustard
$\frac{1}{2}$ cup sunflower oil
Freshly ground black pepper
For the salad:
$2\frac{1}{4}$ pounds vegetables (e.g., red, green and yellow bell peppers,
zucchini, celery, carrots, scallions, romaine lettuce leaves)

Prep time: 1 hour
Per serving (6) approx: 244 calories
4 g protein/21 g fat/14 g carbohydrates

For the herb dip, rinse parsley and basil and remove leaves from stems. Peel garlic. Coarsely chop anchovies, capers, and garlic and add to herbs along with lemon juice. Process all these ingredients finely with a hand blender or food processor while gradually adding olive oil. Stir in breadcrumbs and season dip to taste with salt and pepper.

For the aioli, rinse lemon, grate off zest, and squeeze out juice. Whisk together egg yolk, salt, mustard, and 1 tablespoon lemon juice. First add oil drop by drop, then in a thin stream until the sauce becomes creamy. Season sauce to taste with $\frac{1}{2}$ teaspoon lemon zest, lemon juice, salt, and pepper.

Rinse and clean all vegetables. If desired, peel zucchini and carrots. Depending on size, cut vegetables into halves or quarters and then into strips about 2 inches long. Separate romaine lettuce into leaves, rinse, and spin dry. Arrange all vegetables decoratively on a platter and serve with dips.

TIPS: Depending on what's available, you can combine raw vegetables with those that are briefly blanched. Broccoli and cauliflower florets, Brussels sprouts, and fennel strips go very well with the mayonnaise and herb dip.

You can also serve vegetable crudités with dips as a light appetizer or at a cold buffet.

Lebanese Tomato Salad

Serves 4:

For the dressing:
3 tablespoons walnuts
7 sprigs mint
4 tablespoons extra virgin olive oil
4 tablespoons lemon juice
1 pinch cayenne pepper
1 teaspoon honey
Sea salt
Freshly ground black pepper

For the salad:
4 pieces thin, Middle-Eastern pita bread or lavash
1/3 cucumber
1 green bell pepper
4 beefsteak tomatoes
Sea salt
Freshly ground black pepper
4 sprigs mint
12 black olives
4 romaine lettuce leaves
3 ounces feta

Prep time: 30 minutes
Per serving approx: 438 calories
13 g protein/22 g fat/52 g carbohydrates

Chop walnuts. Rinse mint, remove leaves, and chop. Using a hand blender, process mint, walnuts, oil, lemon juice, cayenne, and honey. The dressing should have the consistency of pesto. Season to taste with salt and pepper (keeps in the refrigerator for up to 2 days).

Heat a wide pan and warm pita bread over low heat without oil. In the meantime, rinse vegetables. Peel cucumber, clean bell pepper, dice both finely, and stir into dressing.

Cut tomatoes in half, remove cores, slice, arrange on plates, and season with salt and pepper. Rinse mint, remove leaves from stems, and place between tomato slices. Distribute walnut vegetable dressing over the tomatoes. Rinse lettuce leaves and spin dry. Cut feta into small pieces. Top pita bread with lettuce and feta, roll up, and cut in half on an angle. Fan out pita bread on platter. Remove pits from olives if desired and use to garnish salad.

Indian Spiced Cauliflower Salad

Serves 4:
Sea salt
12 ounces spinach
6 ounces plain, nonfat yogurt
1 clove garlic
1 teaspoon ground cumin
2 pinches Hungarian hot paprika
1¼ pounds cauliflower florets (from a cauliflower of about 2 pounds)
2 tablespoons sunflower oil
½ teaspoon mustard seeds
½ teaspoon fenugreek seeds (or fennel seeds)
1 pinch chili powder
1 tablespoon cilantro
2 tablespoons lemon juice

Prep time: 30 minutes
Per serving approx: 117 calories
6 g protein/6 g fat/13 g carbohydrates

Bring 2 cups salted water to a boil. Sort spinach, clean, rinse, and add to boiling water. As soon as it starts to wilt (30 seconds), drain, squeeze out well, and chop coarsely.

Combine yogurt and salt in a bowl. Peel garlic, squeeze through a press, and add to yogurt. Season yogurt to taste with cumin and paprika, toss with spinach, and refrigerate.

Rinse cauliflower florets and cut them all to a standard size. In a wide pot, heat oil over medium heat and roast mustard seeds and fenugreek seeds while stirring until they pop.

Add cauliflower and sprinkle with salt and chili powder. Carefully stir cauliflower florets, then braise over low heat for 8–10 minutes, stirring occasionally. (If necessary, add a little more oil.) Let cauliflower cool.

Combine cauliflower and cilantro and sprinkle with lemon juice. Transfer spinach yogurt to a platter or individual bowls and arrange cauliflower on top.

TIP: If the fenugreek and mustard seeds are too strong for your taste, strain the oil before using it to braise the cauliflower.

Mixed Caribbean Salad

Serves 4:
1 small head escarole or oak leaf lettuce
2 tomatoes
1 green bell pepper
1 avocado
1 lime (or 1 lemon)
1 small package garden cress or 1 small bunch watercress
4 ounces unsweetened, canned coconut milk
1 fresh red chile pepper (see tip on page 80)
3 tablespoons crème fraîche
Salt (preferably kosher or sea)
Freshly ground black pepper
Sugar

Prep time: 30 minutes
Per serving approx: 296 calories
3 g protein/27 g fat/15 g carbohydrates

Clean lettuce, rinse, spin dry, and tear into bite-sized pieces. Rinse tomatoes, remove cores, and cut into eighths. Rinse bell pepper, cut into quarters, clean, and cut into fine strips.

Cut avocado in half, remove pit, scoop out the flesh with a large spoon, and cut into narrow wedges. Drizzle avocado with juice squeezed from half of a lime. Rinse and cut cress leaves from stems. Combine all ingredients in a glass or wooden bowl.

Warm coconut milk slightly in a pot and whisk in remaining lime juice. Rinse chile pepper, clean, mince, and stir together with crème fraîche. Remove coconut milk from heat and mix with crème fraîche. Season dressing to taste with salt, pepper, and sugar and pour over the salad.

Salade Niçoise

Serves 4:
9 ounces green beans
Salt (preferably kosher or sea)
8 ounces boiled red potatoes
4 firm tomatoes
1 green bell pepper
1 piece cucumber (about 6 ounces)
1 white onion
1 can tuna (packed in water, 6 ounces drained)
6–8 butterhead lettuce leaves
1 clove garlic
3 tablespoons red wine vinegar
2 teaspoons medium-hot mustard
Freshly ground black pepper
8 tablespoons extra virgin olive oil
10 black olives
1 bunch basil

Prep time: 30 minutes
Per serving approx: 250 calories
13 g protein/17 g fat/15 g carbohydrates

Rinse and clean beans, and cook for 7 minutes in a pot of salted water. Remove beans, rinse under cold water, and drain well.

Peel potatoes and cut into slices about ½-inch thick. Rinse tomatoes, remove cores, and cut into eighths. Rinse bell pepper, cut into quarters, clean, and cut into thin strips. Peel cucumber and dice. Peel onion and slice finely. Drain tuna and separate with a fork. Clean lettuce, rinse, and tear into bite-sized pieces.

Peel garlic and cut in half. Rub garlic on the inside of a bowl. In this bowl, mix together vinegar, mustard, salt, and pepper, then whisk in oil. Add salad ingredients to the vinaigrette and toss well. Pit olives if desired (preferably with a cherry pitter). Rinse basil and sprinkle basil leaves and olives over the salad.

Celery Avocado Salad

Serves 4:
1¼ pounds celery
1 avocado
3 tablespoons white wine vinegar
1 tablespoon pumpkin seed oil
2 tablespoons sunflower oil
1 tablespoon plain yogurt
Sea salt
White pepper
1 bunch mixed herbs (e.g., tarragon, basil, parsley)
Several leaves of iceberg lettuce
2 tablespoons pumpkin seeds

Prep time: 35 minutes
(+30 minutes marinating time)
Per serving approx: 222 calories
4 g protein/20 g fat/12 g carbohydrates

Cut leaves from celery, pull off tough fibers, and rinse. Set aside leaves and slice stalks very thinly on an angle.

Cut avocado in half, remove pit, scoop flesh from peel with a large spoon, and dice. In a blender or with a hand blender, purée avocado, vinegar, both types of oil and yogurt until smooth. Pour avocado purée into a bowl, season with salt and pepper, and mix well with celery. Cover and refrigerate for 30 minutes.

Just before serving, rinse herbs, chop finely, and stir into salad. Season to taste. Roast pumpkin seeds in a pan without oil and let cool. Rinse iceberg lettuce and spin dry. Line four individual bowls with lettuce leaves. Transfer salad to bowls and sprinkle with pumpkin seeds. Garnish with celery greens.

This salad goes well with fresh goat cheese and rye bread.

Serves 4:
10 ounces green beans
10 ounces yellow wax beans
Salt (preferably kosher or sea)
2 sprigs savory or 1 sprig mint and 1 sprig thyme
2 firm pears
2 tablespoons lemon juice
For the dressing:
1 onion
3½ ounces smoked bacon
2 tablespoons vegetable or canola oil
1 tablespoon lemon juice
2 tablespoons raspberry vinegar
Freshly ground black pepper

Prep time: 30 minutes
Per serving approx: 429 calories
21 g protein/17 g fat/52 g carbohydrates

Rinse both types of beans, clean, and cut in half if desired. Bring 1 quart salted water to a boil in each of two pots, put one sprig of savory in each, and place one type of bean in each. Cover and cook beans 6–15 minutes (depending on type) until al dente.

In the meantime, make the dressing. Peel onion and dice finely. Remove rind and any thick gristle from bacon and dice finely. (Partially frozen bacon is much easier to dice.) In a pan, heat oil slightly and brown bacon until crisp. Add diced onion and brown slightly.

Transfer bacon-onion mixture to a bowl and mix thoroughly with lemon juice and fruit vinegar. Season dressing to taste with pepper.

Pour beans into a colander and drain well. Let cool and toss with bacon dressing.

Rinse pears and wipe off thoroughly. Cut pears into quarters, remove seeds, cut quarters into wedges, and immediately sprinkle with lemon juice. Arrange beans and pears together. Grind pepper over the top.

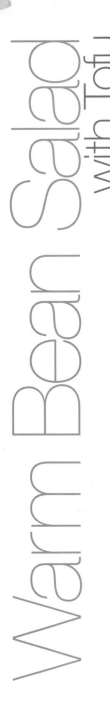

Warm Bean Salad with Tofu

Serves 4:
8 ounces tofu
1 tablespoon chopped rosemary needles
1 bay leaf
4 ounces dry, large lima beans
4 ounces dry kidney beans
Sea salt
2 tablespoons balsamic vinegar
Freshly ground black pepper
5 tablespoons extra virgin olive oil
1 teaspoon thyme leaves
1 tablespoon chopped Italian parsley
1 green bell pepper
2 tomatoes
9 ounces broccoli
1 clove garlic
2 marinated artichoke hearts

Prep time: 1¼ hours
(+1 hour soaking time)
Per serving approx: 347 calories
19 g protein/13 g fat/45 g carbohydrates

Cut tofu into slices ⅓-inch thick and then into sticks and sprinkle with rosemary. Cut bay leaf in half. Bring different types of beans to a boil separately in 1¼ cups salted water with ½ bay leaf each. Boil for 2 minutes, remove from heat, cover, and let stand 1 hour. Then bring each pot of beans to a boil and cook covered over low heat for 45 minutes. After 30 minutes, add salt.

While the beans are cooking, mix vinegar, salt, and pepper and whisk in 3½ tablespoons oil. Add thyme leaves and parsley. Rinse and clean bell peppers and tomatoes. Dice and mix with vinaigrette.

Rinse broccoli and divide into florets. Cut florets lengthwise into thin slices. Peel garlic and chop. Drain artichoke hearts and quarter lengthwise. Keep these ingredients separate and set aside.

Drain beans and toss with vinaigrette. Season to taste with salt and pepper. In a wide pan, heat remaining oil and brown garlic and tofu over low heat for 3 minutes, stirring occasionally. Add artichoke hearts and sliced broccoli and heat thoroughly. Toss loosely with the salad.

TIP: Don't salt the beans for the first 30 minutes to keep the peels from becoming too tough.

Lentil Salad with Pumpkin & Romanesco

Serves 4:
1 clove garlic
8 ounces French lentils
1 bay leaf
2 sprigs parsley
1 sprig thyme
½ bunch chives
1 shallot
4 tablespoons balsamic vinegar (or red wine vinegar)
Sea salt
Freshly ground black pepper
½ cup extra virgin olive oil
1 small carrot
⅓ celery stalk
9 ounces pumpkin
8 ounces romanesco (or broccoli)
4–5 scallions
1 teaspoon vegetable oil
8 slices whole grain baguette
1 bunch watercress

Prep time: 1 hour
Per serving approx: 493 calories
21 g protein/18 g fat/66 g carbohydrates

Peel pumpkin with a sharp knife.

Cut carrots into fine strips, then into tiny cubes.

Grill scallions and bread on a grill pan.

Peel garlic. Bring lentils to a boil in 2½ cups water along with garlic and bay leaf. Remove from heat and let stand 45 minutes.

Rinse parsley and thyme, remove leaves, and chop. Rinse chives and chop. Peel shallot and dice finely. Combine herbs with shallot, vinegar, salt, and pepper. Whisk in oil.

Rinse and clean carrot, celery, pumpkin, and romanesco. Peel carrot and pumpkin. Use only the florets from the romanesco.

Dice all ingredients very finely, toss in the dressing, and let stand.

In the meantime, bring lentils to a boil in their soaking water, cover, and cook over low heat for 5 minutes. Add salt during the last minute of cooking. Drain lentils, add to vegetables and dressing, and toss.

Heat a grill pan over medium heat. Rinse and clean scallions. Brush oil onto grill pan and grill onions and bread for 1 minute on each side. Rinse watercress, spin dry, and remove leaves from stems. Season lentil salad to taste with vinegar, distribute on plates, and garnish with watercress, scallions, and baguette slices.

TIPS: Instead of pumpkin and romanesco, you can also use diced tomatoes and diced green bell peppers.

If you don't have a grill pan, use a sauté pan and cook the scallions and bread in 1 tablespoon oil for about 3 minutes.

Waldorf Salad

Serves 4:
1 egg yolk
3 tablespoons lemon juice
½ cup sunflower or corn oil
3–4 tablespoons heavy cream
Salt (preferably kosher or sea)
Freshly ground black pepper
3 stalks celery
2 ounces walnuts
3 firm tart apples

Prep time: 30 minutes
Per serving approx: 450 calories
3 g protein/42 g fat/18 g carbohydrates

Stir together egg yolk and 1 tablespoon lemon juice in a tall bowl. First add oil drop by drop and then in a thin stream while stirring vigorously until you have a creamy mayonnaise. Stir in cream and season mayonnaise to taste with salt and pepper.

Rinse celery and pull off tough fibers. Remove leaves and set aside for garnish. Slice celery stalks thinly on an angle. Chop walnuts coarsely.

Rinse apples, wipe off thoroughly (or peel if desired), cut into quarters, and remove core. Cut apple into 1-inch cubes and drizzle immediately with remaining lemon juice.

Add celery, walnuts, and apple cubes to mayonnaise and season heartily to taste. Serve garnished with celery greens.

TIP: For a special occasion, sauté 8 raw, peeled, jumbo shrimp in a little oil and minced garlic for 2–3 minutes and arrange on salad. Or mix 5 ounces peeled, cooked shrimp with the other ingredients.

Chinese Cabbage with Lychees

Serves 6:
8 ounces frozen peas
½ Chinese (also called Napa) cabbage (about 1 pound)
8 ounces mung bean sprouts
8 ounces canned bamboo shoots
1 can lychees (10 ounces drained)
2 tablespoons sesame seeds
For the dressing:
1 clove garlic
3 tablespoons raspberry vinegar
4 tablespoons sherry vinegar
1 tablespoon soy sauce
Salt (preferably kosher or sea)
Freshly ground black pepper
¼ teaspoon ground ginger
½ cup sunflower or corn oil
2 tablespoons sesame oil

Prep time: 25 minutes
Per serving approx: 208 calories
6 g protein/14 g fat/16 g carbohydrates

Let peas thaw. Rinse Chinese cabbage, clean, and cut into thin strips. Rinse mung bean sprouts and drain. Cut bamboo shoots into narrow strips.

Drain lychees well and save juice. In a pan, roast sesame seeds without oil and set aside.

For the dressing, peel garlic and squeeze through a press into a bowl. Add vinegar, soy sauce, salt, pepper, and ginger plus 2 tablespoons lychee juice. Mix well, whisk in 2 types of oil, and toss with salad vegetables. Sprinkle salad with sesame seeds.

This salad goes well as a side dish with quick-fried meat or grilled fish or poultry.

TIP: In the winter, you can prepare this salad with fresh lychees, which mainly arrive in the market in December and January. This aromatic, slightly sour fruit is easy to prepare: Break the white, mother-of-pearl-like fruit out of the dark-red shell like an egg and remove the large pit. Figure about 12 ounces fresh lychees for this recipe and simply substitute pineapple juice for the lychee juice.

Poultry and Meat Salads

Chicken Salad with Papaya

Serves 4:
1 quart chicken stock
4 small chicken breasts with rib meat (about 2 pounds)
1 bay leaf
2 papayas
1 can hearts of palm (8 ounces drained)
3 stalks celery
1½ ounces slivered almonds

For the marinade:
6 ounces mayonnaise
6 ounces crème fraîche
1 tablespoon mango or mixed fruit chutney (from a jar)
2 tablespoons chicken stock
½ teaspoon curry powder
Salt (preferably kosher or sea)
White pepper

Prep time: 1 hour
(+2 hours marinating time)
Per serving approx: 682 calories
53 g protein/36 g fat/40 g carbohydrates

In a wide pot, heat chicken stock. Add chicken breasts and bay leaf. If necessary, add a little water. Cover and cook chicken breasts over low heat for 25 minutes until done, then let cool in the stock. Remove breasts from stock.

In the meantime, peel papayas, cut in half lengthwise and remove seeds with a spoon. Cut papaya halves lengthwise into wedges and dice wedges. Drain hearts of palm and cut into ⅓-inch thick slices. Rinse celery, remove leaves, and pull off tough fibers. Cut stalks in half lengthwise and slice finely crosswise.

For the dressing, vigorously stir together mayonnaise, crème fraîche, and mango chutney. Stir in chicken stock, curry, salt, and pepper.

Remove skin from chicken breasts and debone. Cut meat into ½-inch cubes or pieces. Combine meat-papaya mixture and dressing in a serving bowl. Cover and marinate in the refrigerator for 2 hours.

Remove from refrigerator 15 minutes before serving. Roast almonds in a nonstick pan without oil until golden brown. Add seasoning to salad if desired and sprinkle with slivered almonds.

Serves 4:
2 tablespoons lime juice
1 teaspoon honey
2 tablespoons freshly
grated ginger
4 tablespoons extra virgin olive oil
14 ounces chicken breast fillet
Sea salt
Freshly ground black pepper
1 yellow bell pepper
2 tomatoes

1 pineapple
1 tablespoon oil
½ head oak leaf lettuce
1 bunch watercress

Prep time: 40 minutes
Per serving approx:
302 calories
21 g protein/11 g fat/
34 g carbohydrates

Cut pineapple in half lengthwise, then cut each half into 4 wedges.

For the marinade, combine lime juice, honey, and ginger. Whisk in olive oil. Season chicken breast with salt and pepper and brush with 1 tablespoon marinade. Rinse bell pepper, tomatoes, and pineapple. Clean bell pepper, cut into quarters, and brush with marinade. Cut tomatoes in half, remove cores, dice finely, and mix with 2 tablespoons marinade that has been set aside.

Cut pineapple in half lengthwise and cut each half lengthwise into four wedges. Score pineapple flesh on an angle every 1 inch without cutting through the peel. Brush pineapple with remaining marinade.

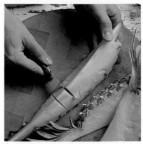

Carefully cut into fruit on an angle at 1-inch intervals without cutting through the peel.

Heat a grill pan over medium heat, brush with oil, and grill chicken breasts for 3–5 minutes on each side. Remove and keep warm. Grill bell pepper with the peel side down for 3 minutes, then cut into smaller pieces and add to tomatoes. Grill pineapple for 3 minutes on each flesh side.

Cut the core (on the narrow side of the wedges) off of 4 pineapple wedges and cut the fruit away from the peel. Add those pineapple chunks to tomatoes and toss together.

Cut the core off of the narrow side of 4 grilled pineapple wedges.

Clean oak leaf lettuce and sort watercress. Rinse lettuce and watercress separately and spin dry. Arrange oak leaf on four plates. Thinly slice chicken breast fillets crosswise against the grain and toss with vegetables.

Distribute chicken mixture on lettuce. Place pineapple wedges with peels on the plates and garnish with watercress. Serve with toasted, dark rye bread.

TIP: You can also cook pineapple, chicken, and vegetables in a sauté pan, but then you'll need more oil: In a pan, heat 2 tablespoons olive oil over medium heat and sauté the chicken breast fillet you brushed with marinade until done, turning once. Then braise bell pepper and pineapple, turning several times. They will require 2–3 more minutes to cook.

Orange Pork & Fennel Salad

Serves 4:
2 oranges
1 large fennel bulb, with greens
9 ounces pork fillet
Salt (preferably kosher or sea)
Freshly ground black pepper
1 tablespoon oil

For the dressing:
2 tablespoons orange marmalade
2 tablespoons raspberry vinegar
Salt (preferably kosher or sea)
Freshly ground black pepper
Cayenne pepper
5 tablespoons extra virgin olive oil

Prep time: 40 minutes
Per serving approx: 269 calories
10 g protein/19 g fat/20 g carbohydrates

Peel oranges, completely removing the white outer membrane. Then peel each section over a bowl or carving board with a groove for catching juices.

Rinse fennel bulb and clean. Set aside greens. Cut bulb in half and cut lengthwise into very fine strips.

Season pork fillet with salt and pepper. In a pan, heat oil until very hot and fry meat quickly on all sides for 2–3 minutes. Then reduce heat and continue frying fillet on all sides for another 6 minutes. Wrap fillet in plastic wrap and aluminum foil and set aside pan and fillet.

For the dressing, put orange marmalade through a sieve if desired. Then mix with raspberry vinegar, salt, pepper, and a little cayenne and whisk in olive oil thoroughly.

Pour orange juice produced when peeling orange sections into the pan used for cooking pork, heat briefly, and stir into juice from the fillet. Stir this mixture into salad dressing and season dressing to taste.

Slice pork fillet and arrange on plates along with orange sections and fennel. Drizzle with dressing and garnish with fennel greens.

TIP: After frying, let the fillet stand before slicing it. The juices will then be distributed evenly and won't run out when you cut into the meat. The result will be nice, juicy slices of pork.

Veal
with Bell Pepper Vinaigrette

Serves 4:
1 quart veal or beef stock
14 ounces veal medallions
Salt (preferably kosher or sea)
Freshly ground black pepper
1 yellow bell pepper
1 red bell pepper

For the marinade:
1 teaspoon medium-hot mustard
2 tablespoons sherry vinegar
1 clove garlic
1 bunch basil
3 tablespoons safflower oil
Salt (preferably kosher or sea)
Lemon pepper
Several green lettuce leaves such as frisée

Prep time: 40 minutes
Per serving approx: 244 calories
26 g protein/13 g fat/5 g carbohydrates

In a pot, heat stock and simmer meat uncovered over low heat for 20 minutes. Remove meat, season with salt and pepper, wrap in plastic wrap, and refrigerate.

Rinse bell pepper, cut in half, and clean. First cut halves lengthwise into narrow strips, then crosswise into very small cubes. Place in a bowl and cover.

For the marinade, mix mustard with vinegar. Peel garlic, squeeze through a press, and add to marinade. Rinse basil and cut leaves into fine strips. Stir in basil and then whisk in oil. Season with salt and lemon pepper. Combine marinade with bell pepper cubes.

With a sharp knife, cut meat crosswise against the grain into paper-thin slices. Rinse lettuce leaves, spin dry, and arrange on a salad platter. Top with veal slices and distribute the prepared bell pepper vinaigrette over the top.

When served with toasted baguette slices, this salad makes a nutritious appetizer.

Basque Lamb Salad

Serves 4:
10–12 ounces cooked lamb
1 can white beans (14 ounces)
1 yellow bell pepper
1 white onion
3 tomatoes
2 ounces pitted green olives
1 bunch Italian parsley
1 bunch basil
4 tablespoons red wine vinegar
Salt (preferably kosher or sea)
Freshly ground black pepper
2 cloves garlic
6–7 tablespoons extra virgin olive oil

Prep time: 30 minutes
Per serving approx: 441 calories
19 g protein/27 g fat/32 g carbohydrates

Cut meat into narrow strips. Drain beans. Rinse bell pepper, cut in half, and clean. First cut halves lengthwise into narrow strips, then crosswise into very small cubes. Peel onion, cut in half, and then into crescents. Rinse tomatoes, remove cores, and dice. Slice olives. Rinse parsley and basil and remove leaves from stems. Set aside a few basil leaves and chop all other herbs.

In a bowl, combine vinegar, salt, and pepper. Peel garlic, squeeze through a press, and whisk into dressing with oil. Toss dressing with lamb, vegetables, and herbs, and garnish with basil leaves.

TIPS: Instead of lamb and white beans, you can use 10 ounces cooked beef and 14 ounces green beans cooked al dente.

If you don't have any meat left over from the day before, you can also use freshly cooked lamb. In this case place 1¼ pounds lean leg of lamb in a pot and cover with cold water. Clean and chop 1 leek and 2 small carrots and add to meat along with ½ teaspoon salt, 5 peppercorns, and 1 bay leaf. Cover and slowly bring to a boil. Simmer gently over low heat for 1 hour. Remove lamb from the pot, let cool and continue as described above.

Beef
with Chile Peppers

Serves 4:
1 quart beef or veal stock
1¾ pounds beef (e.g., rib roast)
1 yellow onion
1 red bell pepper
1 green bell pepper
7 ounces cocktail onions
7 ounces cooked pumpkin pieces (may substitute butternut squash)

For the marinade:
1 piece fresh ginger (about the size of a walnut)
1 clove garlic
2 fresh red chile peppers (see tip below)
2 tablespoons prepared chili sauce
1 tablespoon soy sauce
2 tablespoons balsamic vinegar
2 tablespoons sunflower oil
1 tablespoon sesame oil
Salt (preferably kosher or sea)
Ground allspice
Freshly ground black pepper
1 bunch cilantro

Prep time: 30 minutes
(+1¼ hours simmering time +2 hours marinating time)
Per serving approx: 446 calories
28 g protein/31 g fat/15 g carbohydrates

In a pot, heat stock. Add meat and pour in a little water if necessary (the meat should be covered with liquid). Cover and simmer over low heat for 1–1¼ hours until done, then let cool in the stock.

In the meantime, peel onion, cut in half, and cut crosswise into fine strips. Rinse bell peppers, cut in half and clean, then cut halves lengthwise into thin strips. Drain cocktail onions in a strainer. Cut pumpkin pieces into strips. Place vegetables in a bowl.

For the marinade, peel ginger and garlic and dice finely. Rinse chile peppers, cut in half, and remove seeds. Cut halves lengthwise into fine strips. Vigorously stir together chili sauce, soy sauce, vinegar, and oil. Stir in chile peppers, garlic, and ginger. Season marinade to taste with allspice and pepper.

First cut cooled meat crosswise against the grain into thin slices, then into strips. Combine meat with the prepared vegetables. Pour marinade over the top and mix together well. Then cover with plastic wrap and refrigerate for 2 hours. Remove from refrigerator 15 minutes before serving. Rinse cilantro, remove leaves, and sprinkle over salad.

TIP: When preparing chile peppers, it's best to wear rubber gloves because the heat of the pepper sticks to your fingers even after you wash your hands. In any case, never touch your hands to your eyes or any mucous membrane shortly after handling peppers.

Rabbit Fillet
with Cranberry Yogurt

Serves 4:
12 ounces rabbit fillet
1 teaspoon juniper berries
1 teaspoon dried thyme
Salt (preferably kosher or sea)
Freshly ground black pepper
2 tablespoons vegetable or canola oil
1 head red leaf lettuce
8 dried apricots
For the dressing:
6 ounces plain yogurt
3 tablespoons canned cranberries
2 tablespoons extra virgin olive oil
Salt (preferably kosher or sea)
Freshly ground black pepper

Prep time: 45 minutes
(+2 hours marinating time)
Per serving approx: 347 calories
18 g protein/19 g fat/28 g carbohydrates

Rinse rabbit fillets under cold water and dry. Remove skin and sinew. Chop juniper berries or crush in a mortar and combine with thyme, salt, pepper, and oil. Rub mixture into rabbit fillets, cover, and refrigerate for at least 2 hours.

For the dressing, stir together yogurt, cranberries, and olive oil and season to taste with salt and pepper.

Clean lettuce, rinse, dry thoroughly, tear into bite-size pieces, and arrange on plates. Rinse apricots under hot water, dice finely, and sprinkle over the top.

Heat a pan without oil until very hot and fry marinated rabbit fillets on all sides for 5 minutes until golden brown. Slice on an angle and arrange on salad. Serve dressing on the side.

TIP: After frying, let rabbit fillets stand for 4–5 minutes before cutting into them so the meat will remain moist.

Fish and Seafood Salads

Serves 4:
2 tablespoons lemon juice
Sea salt
Freshly ground black pepper
4 tablespoons extra virgin olive oil
½ cucumber
4 ounces radicchio
½ head oak leaf lettuce
1 bunch sorrel (may substitute arugula)
6 ounces cherry tomatoes
4 slices whole wheat bread
8 slices smoked salmon
Several whole chives

Prep time: 20 minutes
Per serving approx: 186 calories
8 g protein/10 g fat/17 g carbohydrates

For the dressing, mix lemon juice, salt, and pepper in a bowl, then whisk in oil. Peel cucumber, cut in half lengthwise, and shave off strips with a vegetable peeler. Toss with the dressing.

Clean radicchio and oak leaf, separate into leaves, rinse, and spin dry. Sort sorrel, cut off stems, rinse, and spin dry. Then roll up about 10 leaves of sorrel at a time and cut into ½-inch wide strips. Rinse cherry tomatoes and cut in half. Toast bread in a toaster and cut each slice diagonally into 4 triangles. Roll up salmon slices and cut into 1-inch thick rolls.

Remove cucumber from dressing. Dip radicchio and oak leaf into dressing and distribute on plates. Return cucumber to bowl along with sorrel and tomatoes, then distribute on beds of lettuce. Garnish with salmon rolls and chives and place toast triangles around the edges.

TIP: If you want to serve this salad as a small meal, combine it with new potatoes or fried potatoes.

Provençal Fish Salad

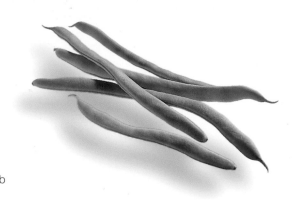

Serves 4:
1¼ pounds red new potatoes
12 ounces green beans
1 sprig savory or mint
Sea salt
1 sprig thyme
1 sprig Italian parsley
3 tablespoons white wine vinegar
Freshly ground black pepper
1 pinch mustard powder
6 tablespoons extra virgin olive oil
8 ounces watercress
14 ounces fish fillet (e.g., rainbow trout, halib
2 cups vegetable stock

Prep time: 45 minutes
Per serving approx: 344 calories
26 g protein/14 g fat/30 g carbohydrates

Rinse potatoes, put in a medium pot, add just enough salted water to cover, and cook for 20–25 minutes. Clean green beans, rinse, and cut in half. Place in a pot of boiling, salted water with savory, and cook for 5–6 minutes. Rinse beans thoroughly with cold water and drain well.

For the salad dressing, rinse thyme and parsley and remove leaves from stems. Finely chop parsley. Mix together vinegar, pepper, salt, and mustard powder. Whisk in oil and mix in thyme and parsley.

Toss beans with salad dressing. Rinse watercress, sort, and cut off larger stems.

Drain potatoes, rinse under cold water, peel, slice, and toss with salad dressing. Remove any bones from fish and cut fillets into ½-inch cubes. Bring vegetable stock to a boil, add fish, cover, and simmer over low heat for 2–3 minutes. Remove fish cubes from stock and carefully stir into salad. Garnish fish salad with watercress.

TIP: It's worth making the vegetable stock yourself because it will then have a finer flavor than anything you buy in the store. You can also make a larger amount and freeze it in batches. For 1 quart vegetable stock, place 14 ounces diced vegetables (e.g., carrots, celery, leek, tomatoes), 1 clove garlic, 1 bay leaf, 1 sprig thyme, 2 sprigs parsley, 1 sprig marjoram, and 1 diced red onion in 1 quart water, cover, and simmer over low heat for 40 minutes. Then pour stock through a strainer.

Marinated Trout Salad

Serves 4:
10 ounces very fresh rainbow trout fillets
1 shallot
1/2 bunch cilantro (may substitute Italian parsley)
1 level teaspoon salt (preferably kosher or sea)
1/2 cup lime or lemon juice
1/2 yellow bell pepper
1 piece zucchini (about 2 ounces)
2 scallions
1 tomato
2 ounces coconut cream (in solid form)
6 tablespoons low fat milk
1 clove garlic
1/4 teaspoon freshly grated ginger
Freshly ground black pepper
Several leaves escarole or iceberg lettuce

Prep time: 30 minutes
(+24 hours marinating time)
Per serving approx: 207 calories
14 g protein/12 g fat/12 g carbohydrates

If necessary, remove skin and bones from fish fillets, dice finely and place in a bowl. Peel shallot and slice finely. Set aside 1–2 cilantro sprigs. Rinse remaining cilantro, remove leaves, and chop coarsely.

Mix cilantro, shallot, and salt with fish. Pour 6–7 tablespoons lime juice over the top. Place a plate on top of the fish and weight the plate down. Marinate fish in the refrigerator for 24 hours, stirring once or twice.

The next day, rinse bell pepper and zucchini, clean, and dice finely. Rinse scallions, clean, and cut into fine rings. Pour boiling water over tomato, peel, remove seeds and core, and dice finely.

For the dressing, grate creamed coconut coarsely with a vegetable grater. Heat milk slightly and dissolve coconut cream while stirring, then remove from heat. Peel garlic, squeeze through a press, and add. Add ginger. Stir together well and season with salt, pepper, and remaining lime juice.

Remove fish from marinade and toss with vegetables and coconut dressing. Rinse lettuce leaves, arrange in bowls or on a platter, and distribute fish salad on top. Rinse remaining cilantro, remove leaves, and use to garnish salad.

Serves 6:
1 cooked lobster
(about 1¼ pounds with shell)
8 ounces frozen peas, thawed
1¾ pounds fresh clams
(or 6 ounces canned clams)
1 cup dry white wine
7 ounces cod fillet
Salt (preferably kosher or sea)
5 tablespoons lemon juice
3 tablespoons sunflower or corn oil
5 ounces cooked, peeled shrimp
1 clove garlic
Freshly ground black pepper
Hungarian sweet paprika

1 small butterhead lettuce
8 ounces cherry tomatoes
2 hard boiled eggs
1 fresh egg yolk
7 ounces sour cream
2 tablespoons tomato ketchup
1–2 teaspoons grated
horseradish (fresh or from a jar)
1 bunch watercress (may use parsley)

Prep time: 1 hour
(+3 hours thawing time)
Per serving approx: 350 calories
32 g protein/15 g fat/
14 g carbohydrates

After they cool a little, remove clams from shells with your fingers.

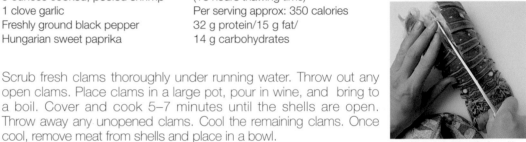
Cut lobster in half lengthwise with a heavy knife.

Remove lobster meat from shell and slice on an angle.

Scrub fresh clams thoroughly under running water. Throw out any open clams. Place clams in a large pot, pour in wine, and bring to a boil. Cover and cook 5–7 minutes until the shells are open. Throw away any unopened clams. Cool the remaining clams. Once cool, remove meat from shells and place in a bowl.

Rinse cod fillets, pat dry, season with salt, and drizzle with 1 tablespoon lemon juice. In a pan, heat 1 tablespoon oil and sauté cod over low heat for 2 minutes on each side. Remove and set aside.

Using a heavy knife, cut lobster in half lengthwise and remove orange vein from tail meat. Remove meat from shell (yields about 6 ounces) and slice.

Cut cod fillet into bite-size pieces and add to bowl with clams. Add lobster meat and shrimp. Sprinkle with 2 tablespoons lemon juice. Peel garlic, squeeze through a press, and add. Toss and season with salt, pepper, and paprika.

Rinse lettuce and shake dry. Arrange leaves on a platter or in a small bowl. Rinse cherry tomatoes and depending on size, cut into halves or quarters. Add peas to fish and seafood in the bowl, toss, and then arrange on lettuce. Peel eggs, quarter, and use to garnish salad.

For the dressing, beat egg yolk and remaining oil until thick and creamy, and gradually work in sour cream. Add remaining lemon juice, tomato ketchup, and horseradish and season with salt and pepper. Pour dressing over salad. Garnish generously with watercress and serve immediately.

TIP: When crawfish are available, you can substitute 8 fresh crawfish at 2 ounces each for the lobster. Prepare a stock of 2 quarts salted water, 3 sprigs parsley, and 1 sliced onion and bring to a rolling boil. Rinse live crawfish under running water, throw into boiling stock, cover, and cook over high heat for 8–10 minutes. Remove the crawfish with a slotted spoon, rinse briefly under cold water, and let cool. Twist off the tail from the rest of the body, pry open shell from the belly side, and remove tail meat. Chop tail meat as desired.

Serves 4:
2 cans tuna packed in water (6 ounces each drained)
9 ounces mushrooms
3 tablespoons lime or lemon juice
6 stalks celery (about 5 ounces)
1 fresh red chile pepper (see tip on page 93)
5 ounces mayonnaise
3 ounces sour cream
1 teaspoon medium-hot mustard
Salt (preferably kosher or sea)
Freshly ground black pepper
1 clove garlic
1 bunch Italian parsley

Prep time: 30 minutes
(+1 hour refrigeration time)
Per serving approx: 320 calories
25 g protein/16 g fat/23 g carbohydrates

Drain tuna in a strainer, transfer to a bowl, and separate with a fork.

Wipe off mushrooms with a dry cloth, clean, and slice thinly or quarter. Drizzle with 2 tablespoons lime juice. Rinse celery, clean, and set aside leaves. Cut stalks in half lengthwise and then into thin slices. Rinse chile pepper, cut in half, clean, and cut into thin strips. Combine all these ingredients with tuna.

Stir together mayonnaise, sour cream, mustard, remaining lime juice, salt, and pepper. Peel garlic, squeeze through a press, and add. Rinse parsley, remove leaves, chop finely, and add to dressing. Toss dressing with tuna, cover, and refrigerate for 1 hour. Garnish with celery greens.

TIP: This salad is intended to serve as a meal for 4 people, with a fresh baguette. However, it can also be served as an appetizer for 6–8 people or as a party salad for a buffet.

Spicy Calamari Salad

Serves 4:
6 ounces small, fresh or frozen squid
6 ounces rockfish fillet
Salt (preferably kosher or sea)
Freshly ground black pepper
2 teaspoons lemon juice
4 tablespoons sunflower or corn oil
1–2 fresh red chile peppers (see tip on page 93)
1 piece fresh ginger (about the size of a walnut)
1 mango, not quite ripe and with flesh removed from pit (about 6 ounces)
4 tablespoons lime juice
1–2 tablespoons fish sauce (see tip below)
Several leaves frisée (optional)
2 tablespoons roasted salted peanuts

Prep time: 30 minutes
(+15 minutes marinating time)
Per serving approx: 218 calories
15 g protein/12 g fat/14 g carbohydrates

Thaw squid if necessary. Season fish fillet with salt and pepper and drizzle with lemon juice. Cut squid into fine rings and season.

In a pan, heat 2 tablespoons oil and fry rockfish fillet on both sides over medium heat for 5 minutes. Remove from pan and set aside. Put squid into leftover oil, add 4 tablespoons water, cover, and braise for 3 minutes. Remove and set aside.

Cut fish fillets into bite-size pieces. Rinse chile peppers, cut in half, clean, and dice finely. Peel ginger and chop finely. Peel mango and grate coarsely (yields about 4 ounces fruit). Carefully mix half the mango with squid, chile peppers, and ginger.

Thoroughly whisk lime juice, fish sauce, and remaining oil, pour over squid, and stir carefully. Then fold in rockfish fillet. If desired, rinse frisée leaves, shake dry, and place on a platter or plates. Arrange fish salad on top. Sprinkle with remaining grated mango. Marinate in refrigerator for 15 minutes. Just before serving, roughly chop peanuts and sprinkle over salad.

TIP: You can find fish sauce at an Asian market or in the specialty department of supermarkets.

Creole Shrimp Salad

Serves 4:
2 tablespoons white wine vinegar
Sea salt
Freshly ground black pepper
1 pinch mustard powder
5 tablespoons extra virgin olive oil
1 orange
1 grapefruit
2 ripe star fruit
1 ripe papaya
½ head green leaf lettuce
12 peeled, cooked jumbo shrimp (about 1 pound)
20 small mint leaves

Prep time: 30 minutes
Per serving approx: 280 calories
25 g protein/12 g fat/20 g carbohydrates

For the dressing, mix vinegar, salt, pepper, and mustard powder in a large bowl and whisk in 4 tablespoons oil.

Rinse fruit and dry. Grate off zest from half the orange and stir into dressing. Using a sharp knife, peel orange and grapefruit over a bowl, also removing the white outer membrane and catching the dripping juice in the bowl.

Quarter both citrus fruits lengthwise and remove white center. Then cut crosswise into ⅓-inch slices and add to dressing. Cut star fruit into ½-inch slices and add to dressing.

Peel papaya, cut in half lengthwise, and scrape out seeds. Then cut crosswise into ⅓-inch slices and add to dressing. Toss dressing and fruit well. Clean lettuce, separate into leaves, rinse, and spin dry.

In a pan, heat remaining oil. Briefly heat shrimp and season with salt and pepper.

Distribute lettuce on plates and top with fruit salad and shrimp. Garnish salad with mint leaves.

Pasta, Potato, and Grain Salads

Pasta Salad with Marinated Vegetables

Serves 4:
6 tablespoons extra virgin olive oil
$\frac{1}{2}$ teaspoon grated lemon zest
1 tablespoon chopped Italian parsley
1 tablespoon chopped rosemary
$\frac{1}{2}$ teaspoon thyme leaves
Sea salt
Freshly ground black pepper
9 ounces zucchini
2 red bell peppers
3 tablespoons lemon juice
14 ounces wheat penne pasta
12 black olives
6 ounces feta

Prep time: 50 minutes
Per serving approx: 582 calories
20 g protein/22 g fat/80 g carbohydrates

Heat a grill pan over medium heat and brush with 1 teaspoon oil. Mix lemon zest, parsley, rosemary, thyme, salt, and pepper, and whisk in remaining oil. Rinse vegetables and clean. Cut zucchini lengthwise into slices about $\frac{1}{2}$-inch thick, brush with a little marinade, grill for 2 minutes on each side, and let cool. Cut bell peppers into quarters, brush with marinade, grill with the peel side down for 3 minutes without turning, and let cool.

Combine remaining marinade with lemon juice. Cut zucchini and bell peppers into pieces about $\frac{1}{2}$-inch thick and place in the marinade.

In the meantime, bring 2 quarts salted water to a boil and cook pasta according to the directions on the package until barely al dente. In the meantime, remove pits from olives (preferably with a cherry pitter) and crumble feta.

Drain pasta and toss with marinated vegetables. Season to taste with salt and pepper. Garnish salad with olives and feta. Serve warm or cold.

Warm Pasta Salad with Lentils

Serves 4:
1 clove garlic
5 ounces French lentils
1 bay leaf
3 tablespoons balsamic vinegar
2 tablespoons light soy sauce
Sea salt
Freshly ground black pepper
1 pinch mustard powder
1 tablespoon thyme leaves
4 tablespoons extra virgin olive oil
2 scallions
4 ounces celery
2 firm ripe tomatoes
12 ounces millet pasta (may substitute wheat flour pasta)
2 ounces sorrel (may substitute arugula)

Prep time: 1 hour
(+1–1½ hours soaking time)
Per serving approx: 459 calories
20 g protein/9 g fat/78 g carbohydrates

Peel garlic. Boil lentils with garlic and bay leaf in 2½ cups water for 2 minutes, remove from heat, and let soak 1–1½ hours.

For the dressing, combine vinegar, soy sauce, salt, pepper, mustard powder, and thyme. Whisk in oil. Rinse onions, clean, chop, and mix into dressing. Rinse celery and tomatoes. Remove leaves and pull off tough fibers from celery and slice stalks thinly. Remove cores from tomatoes and cut into small cubes. Toss celery and tomatoes with dressing and let stand.

In the meantime, bring 2 quarts salted water to a boil and cook pasta according to the directions on the package. After the lentils are done soaking, cover and simmer over low heat for 10–12 minutes. Rinse sorrel, cut off stems, spin dry, and cut into strips. To do so, stack about 10 leaves on top of one another and roll them up. Make cuts at short intervals before unrolling them.

Drain pasta and toss with vegetable vinaigrette. Drain lentils and stir in to pasta. Season salad to taste with salt and pepper and just before serving, gently toss with sorrel.

TIP: If desired, garnish salad with a few iceberg lettuce leaves and celery greens.

Warm Potato & Escarole Salad

Serves 4:

3 tablespoons lemon juice
Sea salt
Freshly ground black pepper
4 tablespoons extra virgin olive oil
2 tablespoons capers
1 tablespoon chopped chives
1 teaspoon thyme leaves
2 tablespoons chopped Italian parsley
½ medium red onion
1¾ pounds long, white potatoes (may substitute red potatoes)
1 clove garlic
1 bay leaf
1 head escarole
4 sun-dried tomatoes
3 ounces Roquefort

Prep time: 45 minutes
Per serving approx: 318 calories
11 g protein/14 g fat/41 g carbohydrates

Combine 2 tablespoons lemon juice with salt and pepper. Stir in 3½ tablespoons oil along with capers and herbs. Peel onions, slice thinly, and marinate in the dressing.

Rinse potatoes and without peeling, barely cover with salted water. Peel garlic and add along with bay leaf and remaining lemon juice to potatoes. Cover and simmer potatoes for 20 minutes until barely done, then drain, peel, cut into slices about ½-inch thick, and toss with salad dressing.

Clean escarole, separate into leaves, rinse, and spin dry. Heat remaining oil slightly. Cut tomatoes into strips, heat in oil, and remove. Tear escarole into bite-size pieces, stir around in the pan once, and fold into potato salad along with tomatoes. Crumble cheese on top.

TIP: When making salads and other dishes that require potatoes to keep their shape when tossed with other ingredients, high moisture, low starch potatoes work best. Try round, white potatoes (Katahdin) or red potatoes.

Potato Artichoke Salad

Serves 4:
1¼ pounds red potatoes
3 sprigs basil
2 sprigs Italian parsley
2 tablespoons balsamic vinegar
Sea salt
Freshly ground black pepper
½ teaspoon thyme leaves
4 tablespoons extra virgin olive oil
4 marinated artichoke hearts
8 ounces cherry or plum tomatoes
16 large, smooth, dark-violet olives
1 ounce goat cheese

Prep time: 45 minutes
Per serving approx: 336 calories
9 g protein/19 g fat/37 g carbohydrates

Cut open olives with a knife and remove pits.

Rinse potatoes and without peeling, cook in salted water for 20–25 minutes until barely done.

In the meantime, make the vinaigrette. Rinse 2 sprigs basil and parsley, remove leaves, and chop. Mix vinegar, salt, pepper, basil, parsley, and thyme and then stir in oil.

Spread a little goat cheese in the pitted olives.

Drain artichoke hearts and quarter lengthwise. Rinse tomatoes and cut in half or quarter.

Drain potatoes, peel, and cut into slices about ¼-inch thick. Arrange artichoke heart quarters, tomato slices, and potato slices on a platter. Pour vinaigrette over the top. Heat a pan slightly.

Squeeze olives gently between your thumb and index finger to loosen the pits. Slit open olives with a paring knife.

Place stuffed olives in the pan and heat.

Remove pits from olives and fill each with a little goat cheese. Place olives in the pan, cover, and heat for about 3 minutes. The cheese should be warm but not melting.

Garnish potato salad with olives. Rinse remaining sprigs basil, shake dry, and garnish salad with the leaves.

TIPS: Instead of stuffed olives, you can serve this salad with toasted slices of whole grain baguette spread with goat cheese.

You can also arrange this colorful salad on a bed of lettuce. To do so, clean 2 ounces arugula, ½ head escarole, and 1 small head radicchio, rinse, and spin dry. Arrange leaves on 4 plates and distribute salad on top.

Use longer, narrow potatoes for your salad so the slices will be nice and bite-sized.

Potato Salad with Olives

Serves 4:
1½ pounds red or fingerling potatoes
Salt (preferably kosher or sea)
2 ounces pitted green olives
2 ounces whole black olives
1 yellow onion
1 red bell pepper
¼ cup vegetable stock

For the marinade:
1 teaspoon medium-hot mustard
2 tablespoons balsamic vinegar
4 tablespoons extra virgin olive oil
2 cloves garlic
1 tablespoon capers
Freshly ground black pepper
Nutmeg
1 can tuna packed in water
(6 ounces drained)

Prep time: 40 minutes
(+30 minutes marinating time)
Per serving approx: 249 calories
13 g protein/11 g fat/26 g carbohydrates

Rinse potatoes and without peeling, cook in salted water for 15–20 minutes until barely done. Then drain and wait until cool enough to handle.

In the meantime, cut green olives in half. Remove pits from black olives (preferably with a cherry pitter) and cut in half. Peel onion, cut in half crosswise, and cut halves into narrow strips. Rinse bell pepper, cut in half, and clean. First cut halves into strips and then into 1-inch cubes. Combine olives, onion, and pepper.

Peel and slice potatoes. Pour vegetable stock over the potatoes.

For the marinade, vigorously whisk together mustard, vinegar, and olive oil. Peel garlic, squeeze through a press, and add to marinade. Chop capers and add. Season marinade with salt, pepper, and a little nutmeg. Combine olive mix with potatoes, pour marinade over the top, and toss carefully. Cover and marinate for 30 minutes.

Drain tuna, separate coarsely with a fork, and fold into salad.

Serve with spicy farm bread or flatbread.

Potato Avocado Salad

Serves 4:
1½ pounds red potatoes
Salt (preferably kosher or sea)
2 shallots
½ cup vegetable stock
2 ripe avocados
1 lemon
1 handful sorrel leaves (may substitute arugula)
2 tablespoons white wine vinegar
3 tablespoons sunflower oil
6 ounces nonfat yogurt
6 ounces crème fraîche
Freshly ground black pepper
2 tablespoons sunflower seeds
1 sprig mint

Prep time: 45 minutes
Per serving approx: 478 calories
8 g protein/37 g fat/34 g carbohydrates

Rinse potatoes and without peeling, cook in salted water for 15–20 minutes until barely done.

Peel shallots and dice finely. Heat vegetable stock and simmer shallots uncovered over low heat for 5 minutes. Drain potatoes, peel, and cut into ½-inch slices. Pour shallots and vegetable stock over potatoes, cover, and let stand.

Squeeze juice from lemon. Cut avocados in half lengthwise and remove pit. Scoop out flesh with a spoon and cut lengthwise into quarters. Slice quarters crosswise and mix immediately with lemon juice.

For the dressing, rinse sorrel leaves, shake dry, and cut into narrow strips. Stir together vinegar, oil, yogurt, and crème fraîche until smooth. Season with salt and pepper. Stir in sorrel strips.

In a pan without oil, roast sunflower seeds for 2–3 minutes. Rinse mint and remove leaves. Toss the prepared salad dressing with potatoes. Carefully fold in avocados. Season to taste with salt and pepper. Just before serving, sprinkle salad with roasted sunflower seeds and mint leaves.

Camargue Rice Salad

Serves 4:
Sea salt
8 ounces whole-grain rice
2 ounces currants
2 sprigs oregano
3 tablespoons lemon juice
Freshly ground black pepper
½ teaspoon grated lemon zest
5 tablespoons extra virgin olive oil
2 ears of white corn
8 asparagus spears
1 small eggplant (9 ounces)
2 ounces pine nuts
3 tablespoons rice wine vinegar
4 tablespoons grape seed oil
¼ teaspoon cinnamon
1 bunch Italian parsley

Prep time: 1 hour
Per serving approx: 455 calories
11 g protein/16 g fat/74 g carbohydrates

Bring 2 cups salted water to a boil. Add rice, cover, and cook over low heat for 40 minutes. In the meantime, cover currants with hot water and let soak. Rinse oregano and chop leaves. Mix lemon juice, salt, pepper, oregano, and lemon zest and whisk in 4 tablespoons oil.

Rinse corn, asparagus, and eggplant. Cut each ear of corn once lengthwise and once crosswise into 4 pieces. Peel the lower half of the asparagus, cut in half crosswise, and then cut lengthwise. Clean eggplant and cut into ½-inch thick slices. Brush vegetables with half the lemon dressing.

Heat a grill pan over medium heat and brush with 1 tablespoon oil. Grill eggplant slices for 2 minutes on each side, remove and keep warm. Then grill asparagus 2–3 minutes on each side, then corn cobs for 6–10 minutes while turning. Season with salt and pepper and keep warm. Mix currants into rice 3 minutes before the end of the cooking time. Heat a pan without oil and roast pine nuts until golden brown.

Drain rice if necessary. Combine remaining lemon dressing, rice vinegar, grape seed oil, and cinnamon. Rinse parsley and chop leaves. Mix rice with parsley and dressing and add seasoning to taste. Sprinkle salad with pine nuts and garnish with grilled vegetables.

TIP: If you use a sauté pan instead of a grill pan, use 2 more tablespoons of oil and extend the cooking time by 1–2 minutes.

Rice Salad with Polish Sausage

Serves 4:
3 small fresh red chile peppers (see tip on page 93)
½ cup vegetable stock
8 ounces long-grain rice
1⅔ cups tomato juice
Salt (preferably kosher or sea)
Freshly ground black pepper
7 ounces spicy Polish sausage
3 tablespoons olive oil
1 clove garlic
4 tablespoons red wine vinegar
3 plum tomatoes
2 scallions

Prep time: 45 minutes
(+1 hour marinating time)
Per serving approx: 423 calories
10 g protein/16 g fat/60 g carbohydrates

Rinse chile peppers, cut in half crosswise, remove seeds, and slice thinly. In a pot, bring vegetable stock to a boil. Add rice and briefly bring to a boil. Add tomato juice and chile peppers to rice, season with salt and pepper, cover tightly, and cook over very low heat for 15–20 minutes until al dente. Let cool.

If desired, peel sausage, then cut on an angle into ½-inch thick slices. In a pan, heat oil and brown sausage slices briefly on both sides. Peel garlic, squeeze through a press, and add. Remove pan from heat and add vinegar. Toss sausage with rice and let stand for 1 hour.

Rinse tomatoes, cut into quarters, and remove cores and seeds. Rinse scallions, clean, and cut on an angle into rings.

To serve, mix some of the tomatoes and scallions into the rice. Season rice to taste with salt and pepper. Garnish rice with remaining tomatoes and scallions.

Mexican-Style Rice Salad

Serves 4:
1 cup vegetable stock
5 ounces long-grain rice
6 ounces canned corn
6 ounces canned kidney beans
1 ripe avocado
2 tablespoons lime juice
2 small firm tomatoes
For the dressing:
2 small fresh red chile peppers (see tip on page 93)
2 tablespoons lime juice
Salt (preferably kosher or sea)
Freshly ground black pepper
5 tablespoons sunflower or corn oil
Cilantro

Prep time: 30 minutes
Per serving approx: 379 calories
7 g protein/17 g fat/55 g carbohydrates

In a pot, bring vegetable stock to a boil. Add rice, cover, and cook over low heat for 20 minutes until al dente.

In the meantime, pour corn and kidney beans into a strainer, rinse under cold water, and drain well.

For the dressing, rinse chile peppers, cut in half, remove seeds, and chop finely. Whisk peppers together with lime juice, salt and pepper, then whisk in oil. Rinse cilantro, chop, and stir into dressing.

Pour rice through a strainer, rinse under cold water, and drain well. In a bowl, toss rice with corn, kidney beans, and dressing.

Cut avocado in half lengthwise and remove pit. Scoop flesh out with a large spoon, cut into ½-inch cubes, and drizzle with lemon juice. Carefully stir into salad.

Rinse tomatoes, cut in half, remove cores, dice finely, and sprinkle on salad.

Good as a side dish with roast or fried chicken.

TIP: Garnish with tortilla chips, iceberg lettuce, and chile peppers.

Oats with Fresh Fruit

Serves 4:
8 ounces rolled oats
1 tart apple
1 orange
4 tablespoons lemon juice
2 ripe mangoes
1 fresh red chile pepper
(see tip on page 93)
2 tablespoons orange juice
Sea salt
Freshly ground black pepper
1½ tablespoons extra virgin olive oil
Cayenne pepper

1 tablespoon fresh, finely chopped mint
1 tablespoon finely chopped Italian parsley
1 banana
1 head white endive
1½ ounces chopped pistachios
1 lemon

Prep time: 50 minutes
(+30 minutes soaking time)
Per serving approx:
289 calories
12 g protein/9 g fat/
66 g carbohydrates

Cut through the mango lengthwise to the left and right of the pit.

First cut into mango lengthwise and then crosswise at 1/2- inch intervals.

Turn grilled mango pieces inside out making the fruit easier to cut away and eat.

In a pot, bring oats to a boil in 2 cups water, cover, and cook over low heat for 30 minutes.

In the meantime, rinse and dry apple and orange. Peel orange, completely removing the white outer membrane, and divide into sections. Peel the apple, remove core, and cut into wedges. Drizzle with 2 tablespoons lemon juice. Heat a grill pan over medium heat.

Rinse mangoes, dry, cut in half lengthwise, and cut away pit. Cut into flesh first lengthwise and then crosswise at ¼-inch intervals to form a diamond pattern, being careful not to cut through the peel. Then cut mango pieces in half lengthwise.

Rinse chile pepper, dry, cut in half lengthwise, and remove seeds. Combine remaining lemon juice with the orange juice, salt, pepper, 1 tablespoon oil, cayenne pepper, mint, and parsley. Cut remaining fruit from mango pit, dice, and add to dressing.

Brush grill pan or a large sauté pan with remaining oil and grill apple wedges, orange sections, chile pepper, and mango quarters. Grill apple and orange for 1 minute on each side. Grill mango quarters with the flesh side down and chile pepper with the peel side down for about 2 minutes.

Drain oats. Peel banana, slice, and stir into oats along with dressing. Separate endive into leaves, rinse, spin dry, chop, and toss with salad. Chop half the grilled apples and oranges and toss with salad. Cut chile pepper into fine strips and add to salad.

Season salad to taste and distribute on plates. Sprinkle salad with pistachios. Garnish with remaining apples and oranges. Turn mango quarters inside out so the fruit cubes stick out from the peel. Cut lemon into eighths and serve lemon wedges and mangoes with salad.

TIP: If you like eating fresh fruit, skip the grill pan and mix the raw fruit into the oats. In this case add only the cubes from 1 mango and toss the oats with all the dressing.

Tabbouleh with Arugula

Serves 4:
8 ounces bulgar wheat
2 cups vegetable stock
4 ounces red onions
1 bunch arugula
1 bunch parsley
3 sprigs mint
4 tablespoons lemon juice
Sea salt
Freshly ground black pepper
4 tablespoons extra virgin olive oil
3 ripe tomatoes
4 leaves baby red leaf lettuce
1 lemon (optional)

Prep time: 30 minutes
Per serving approx: 344 calories
16 g protein/13 g fat/65 g carbohydrates

Bring bulgar wheat and vegetable stock to a boil while stirring. Remove from heat, cover pot, and let stand for 15–20 minutes. Then drain if necessary.

In the meantime, peel onions and dice finely. Rinse arugula, parsley, and mint and spin dry. Set aside half the arugula and chop the other half along with the herbs. Stir chopped ingredients into bulgar.

Mix lemon juice, salt, and pepper, then whisk in oil. Pour dressing over bulgar wheat, toss, and season to taste with salt and pepper. Rinse tomatoes, cut in half, remove cores, dice finely, and toss with salad.

Rinse lettuce leaves, spin dry, tear into bite-size pieces, and arrange on plates along with remaining arugula. Distribute tabbouleh on top. If desired, rinse lemon, dry, cut into wedges, and include with salad.

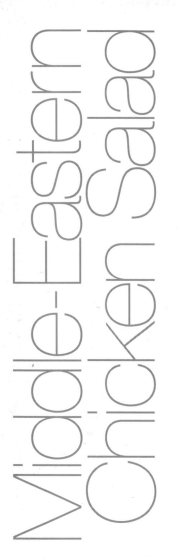

Serves 4:
4 shallots
2 cloves garlic
2 tablespoons oil
2 tablespoons pine nuts
8 ounces long-grain rice
Salt (preferably kosher or sea)
Freshly ground black pepper
1 quart chicken stock
2 tablespoons currants
1⅓ pounds chicken breasts with rib meat
1 bay leaf
3 scallions
3 stalks celery
1 carrot
3 tablespoons lemon juice
½ teaspoon ground cumin
2 pinches cinnamon
3–4 sprigs fresh mint

Prep time: 1 hour
(+1 hour refrigeration time)
Per serving approx: 311 calories
26 g protein/6 g fat/40 g carbohydrates

Peel shallots and garlic and dice finely. In a wide pot, heat oil and sauté shallots and garlic until translucent. Stir in pine nuts and rice and sauté for 3 minutes while stirring until all grains are shiny. Season with salt and pepper. Pour in half the stock, add currants, cover, and cook over low heat for 25–30 minutes. Let cool.

In the meantime, add meat and bay leaf to remaining stock, bring to a boil, cover, and simmer over low heat for 20–25 minutes. Let cool slightly, then remove meat from pot, remove skin, debone, and cut into small pieces. Rinse and clean scallions and celery. Cut scallions into fine rings and celery into thin slices. Peel carrot and grate coarsely.

Season rice with lemon juice, cumin, cinnamon, salt, and pepper. Rinse mint and remove leaves. Set aside several leaves for garnish and chop the rest coarsely. Stir mint, meat, and vegetable ingredients into rice and refrigerate for 1 hour. Just before serving, garnish salad with mint.

TIP: Also tastes great with dressing made from 6 ounces plain yogurt, 2 tablespoons mayonnaise, 1 teaspoon harissa (hot Middle-Eastern chili paste—or use another chili sauce), 3–4 tablespoons lemon juice, salt, and pepper. Just before serving, pour over salad and then garnish with mint.

Index